CW01637948

from Stanhope

By

Keven Shevels

TRAIL GUIDES publications

First published in Great Britain in 2009 by Trailguides Limited.
Second edition published in Great Britain in 2011 by Trailguides Limited.
www.trailguides.co.uk

ISBN 978-1-905444-46-5

Trailguides Limited
35 Carmel Road South
Darlington
Co Durham DL3 8DQ

Cover design by Steve Gustard

CONTENTS

Cover photos.
Front. Looking at Collier Law from Fatherley Hill Currick.
Walk 4 Fatherley Hill.
Back. Walking the Weardale Way along the valley floor.
Walk 5 Rookhope Circular.

INTRODUCTION

1. Stanhope.

Stanhope is known as the capital of Weardale but as with all towns and villages in the dale it will have evolved from one of the small scattered farmsteads that were the early settlements in the dale. Although the first traces of habitation have long disappeared beneath the current buildings the original location was in the best position to establish a farmstead. In Weardale this meant on the south-facing slope of the valley above the flood plain of the River Wear but close to a tributary stream that could provide clean, fresh water. In the case of Stanhope this would mean close to the Stanhope Burn.

The name Stanhope itself is derived from two Old English elements "Staen" meaning stony and "Hop" meaning side valley. Originally this name of "stony side valley" will have applied to the valley of the Stanhope Burn but at some point will have transferred across to the settlement.

Early references to Stanhope were made in the Boldon Book which was Durham's equivalent of the early Norman Doomsday Book which only extended as far north as the River Tees. The Boldon Book was drawn up in 1183 and listed the land holdings of the Bishop of Durham. Within the book Stanhope was listed as having a population of 230 in 47 households and despite being over a hundred years after the conquest many of the inhabitants still had Anglo-

The church of St Thomas dating back to the year 1200 and sometimes known as the little "Cathedral of the Dale".

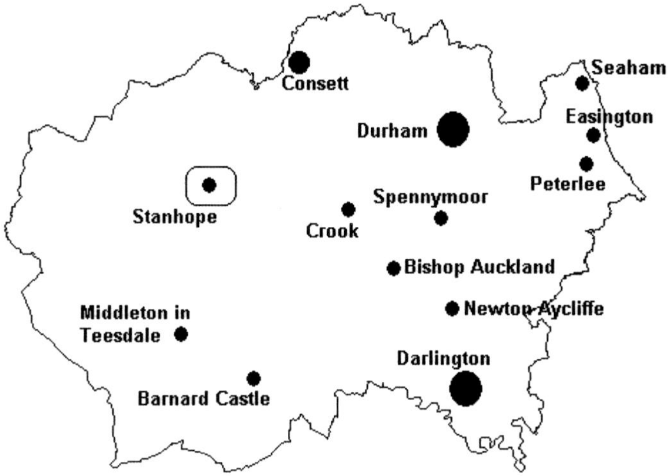

Saxon names such as Gamell, Godric and Meldred. The book painting a picture of a well-established village.

By 1421 Stanhope had developed into a market town with a market place along the main road or Front Street as it is known. The exploitation of lead from the 16th century onwards triggered a growth in the population of the dale and Stanhope was no exception. A survey of 1797 gave a population of 3,600. However it was in the 19th century and the coming of the railways that allowed the large-scale quarrying of limestone which provided the biggest boom to population growth. New employment was created with new housing needed for the workers and Stanhope grew significantly.

However exploitation of natural resources can not last forever and the lead industry had virtually ceased by the start of the 20th century and limestone quarrying was soon to follow. With the decline of industry the importance of tourism has increased and nowadays many of the residents of Stanhope and other parts of the dale commute towards the eastern side of the county for employment.

2. Access & the Right to Roam

The area surrounding Stanhope is a mixture of low and high moorland on the upper slopes of the dale and the more cultivated farmland within the dale itself. As with most upland areas this gives a mixture of access rights with access in the lower farmed areas being legally restricted only to public rights of way such as footpaths and bridleways and this is reflected in those routes in this book that cross this lower part of the valley.

Since with the implementation of the Countryside Right of Way Act 2000 in 2005 and the introduction of the "Right to Roam" this has now changed some access rights and certain upland areas of this part of Weardale have now become legally accessible. This legislation allows walkers the right to roam at will over "designated access land" without the need to be restricted to official footpaths and bridleways.

The CRoW Act has allowed many areas on the moors surrounding Stanhope to be now legally accessible. In this case the trig point on Crow Coal Hill which overlooks Stanhope.

On the new editions of the Ordnance Survey Explorer maps, this new access land is marked with a light yellow coloured background and at the entry points to this land, the stiles and gates carry the new "access land" waymarking symbol of a brown stick man in a brown circle.

The details that accompany each of the walk descriptions will provide information as to whether the route uses rights of way or crosses open access land.

With the right to access has also come responsibility and the walker is expected to observe various limits and restrictions that are placed on their activities at certain times of the year. The landowner and/or farmer has the right to exclude access for up to twenty eight days per year and this is normally applied between May and early July with the breeding season of the ground-nesting birds on the moors. Where they are known, restrictions that may impinge on any given walk are shown in the details for that walk. However, don't take it for granted that these are going to be accurate as each year these restrictions may change. Always check any notices that are placed at the access points for any restrictions. To find out more about out the `right to roam` and whether any general or specific restrictions apply to any part of Weardale then a visit to the website **www.countrysideaccess.gov.uk** will give you all the necessary information.

With using the right to roam and moving away from the recognised footpaths and bridleways, the walker does become more exposed to potential hazards. As with most parts of the North Pennines, Weardale has been heavily exploited for its mineral wealth and this can be clearly seen in the number of old quarry workings that are visible from these walks. This has left a legacy of old workings, quarries and shafts all of which can be hazardous. Caution must always be exercised when in the vicinity of any of these sites.

3. The Walks

The walks in this book are designed to showcase the country and history of the area around Stanhope and to explore the woods, hills and moors surrounding this small town. The walks all start at Stanhope Market Place opposite the church of St Thomas. Cars can be parked here although there is alternative parking along the main street and also in the Durham Dales Centre.

By starting from one specific location such as Stanhope there may be some duplication within the walks particularly as you exit and re-enter the town at the

The Market Place, the start of all the walks in this book.

start and finish of a walk. However this has been kept to a minimum and where one walk does share part of a route with another then that is only for a short distance.

4. The Weather

Although not as high as some of the hills further up Weardale, the hills surrounding Stanhope can still be very exposed and the weather highly changeable. Even in summer it is always advisable to carry a waterproof and some form of warm clothing. Despite global warming there is still a strong prospect of snow during the winter months and whereas the majority of the tracks are easily followed during most of the year, if there is a layer of snow this can make some of them extremely difficult to follow.

5. The Maps

Stanhope is one of those unfortunate locations that fall on the edge of a map, being on the bottom of OL 307 and on the top of OL 31. This means that to cover the whole area of these walks both of these maps are required. Each of the walks in this book has been designed so that they fall within the bounds of the one map enabling the walker to carry just that one relevant map at a time. Within the details of each walk the name of the relevant map is listed.

The full names of the two maps that cover that part of Weardale relevant to these walks are:
Ordinance Survey Explorer OL31 North Pennines Teesdale & Weardale.
Ordinance Survey Explorer OL 307 Consett & Derwent Reservoir.

Any diagrams and route descriptions included in this book are meant as a guide, they are not intended to replace the use of the relevant map. Do not venture onto the hills with just this guide book and no map.

6. Towns, Villages & Accommodation

Within Stanhope and the surrounding villages of Frosterley, Eastgate and Westgate there is a choice of accommodation ranging from small hotels, guest houses, self catering cottages and caravan/camping sites plus a range of facilities such as pubs, shops, cafes and places to eat out.
The Durham Dales Centre, see below, will be happy to assist with any specific requirements.

A couple of the walks in this book require the ability to navigate over open moorland. Here heading towards the high ground of Carrs Top.

7. Tourist Information Centres & Websites

There is just the one visitor centre in the whole of Weardale which is based in Stanhope at the Durham Dales Centre.

Durham Dales Centre, Castle Gardens, Stanhope, Weardale, Co Durham. DL13 2FJ

Telephone 01388 527650.

The centre is open 7 days a week, but times vary through the year dependent upon season.

In addition to the TIC, the Dales Centre hosts other facilities such as tea room, craft shops and conference facilities.

The majority of Weardale lies within the North Pennines Area of Outstanding Natural Beauty. Although the AONB does not operate any visitor centres in Weardale they do organise activities throughout the North Pennines including Weardale and have a very useful website giving information on flora, fauna, geology, attractions and events in the North Pennines. The website can be found at **www.northpennines.org.uk**

8. Stanhope in the Prehistoric

As with many places in this country there is evidence that the area around Stanhope was occupied long before the Romans came to this shore. As for the Romans it appears that they didn't really leave much of a footprint within Weardale instead preferring to leave the area wild and treat it as a hunting estate, see the piece on the Eastgate Roman Altar. However it does seem that the native population were both wealthy, successful and had inhabited the area long before the invaders from Italy..

Unfortunately the industrial scale plundering of the mineral wealth of the dale during the 18th, 19th and into the 20th centuries has probably destroyed much of what was left by our prehistoric ancestors but enough tantalising pieces have been left to suggest an established, prosperous and wealthy society was living here at various locations down from the Stone Age, through the Bronze Age and into the Iron Age and the coming of the Romans.

The walks in this book visit a number of locations where there is evidence of the prehistoric past including field boundaries and the site of the legendary Heathery Burn Hoard. One of the most enigmatic of these is on the first walk "Crow Coal Hill" and passed on the ridgeline leading towards Long Hill.

Set along the ridge are three large mounds, the first with a cairn on top, the second with a sheepfold and the third with another cairn. The probability is that these three mounds are all that is left of three Bronze Age burial mounds. No

The oldest inhabitant of Stanhope. This fossilised tree was part of a great forest that grew on what is now the moorland above Stanhope during the Middle Carboniferous period 250 million years ago. It was found during quarrying operations near to Edmundbyers Cross and brought to Stanhope where it was erected in the grounds of St Thomas' Church in 1962.

excavation has ever been undertaken on them but their appearance and positioning suggest that this is the case. During the later stages of the Bronze Age one of the burial rites practised was to lay the dead beneath a large pile of stones on an elevated position such as a ridge line or hill top. With the size of some of these mounds this was quite a labour intensive ritual and so it is thought to have been reserved only for those with high status such as a king or chief. However it is also thought that these mounds may also have had a duel role in that they not only honour the dead but they also mark out the territory of the people who built them and stated that this tribe had the wealth and power to build these tombs for their dead. The mounds are not just placed on the top of a ridge or hill but they are placed in such a position so as to be visible from a very large distance. Indeed these three mounds even after sitting on the ridge top for four thousand years are still visible from the B6278 as it runs over the moors after leaving Stanhope. Think how visible and impressive they would have been when still relatively newly built and undiminished by time.

9. The Second Battle of Stanhope

This incident was not so much a military conflict as happened between the soldiers of England and Scotland at Stanhope Park but more of an affray between tenant and landowner over tenant's rights. The tenants being the lead miners and farmers of Stanhope and the landowner being Shute Barrington the Bishop of Durham.

When times were hard the local population of Weardale had always regarded it as a right to take game birds from the woods and moors to supplement the pot. Unfortunately the Bishop had a different persuasion and regarded such activities as poaching and issued warnings to the dales folk that these actions would have to stop.

Things came to a head in 1818 when the Bishop sent a force of gamekeepers into the upper dale to arrest the suspected ringleaders of the poaching. This was done and the accused were arrested and temporarily imprisoned in the local inn, the Black Bull. With the arrests a large and angry crowd quickly assembled outside the inn demanding the release of the held men. It didn't take long for this situation to develop into violence during which the Bishop's gamekeepers came out a very poor second. Although no-one was actually killed there was supposedly a great deal of bloodshed and one unfortunate man lost an eye.

This bloody event became known as the Battle of Stanhope and is commemorated in the local ballad "The Bonny Moor Hen", the opening verses of which are below.

The Bonny Moor Hen

The account of a battle you quickly shall here,
That was fought by the miners, so well you may ken
By claiming a right to the bonny moor hen.
Oh this bonny moor hen, as it plainly appears,
She belonged to their fathers some hundreds of years;
But the miners of Weardale are all valiant men,
They will fight till they die for their bonny moor hen.
Oh the miners in Weardale, they are bred to the game,
They level their pieces and make sure of their aim;
When the shot it goes off - Oh, the powder doth sing,
They are sure to take off, a leg or a wing
Now, the times being hard and provisions being dear,
The miners were starving almost we do hear;
They had nought to depend on, so well you may ken,
But to make what they could of their bonny moor hen.
There's the fat man of Auckland and Durham the same
Lay claim to the moors and likewise the game
They send word to the miners they would have them to ken
They would stop them from shooting the bonny moor hen.
Of these words they were carried to Weardale with speed
Which made the poor miners hang down their heeds
But then sent an answer they would have them to ken
They would fight till they died for their bonny moor hen.
When this answer it came to the gentlemen's ears,
An army was risen, it quickly appears;
Land stewards, bum bailiffs, and game-keepers too
Were all ordered to Weardale to fight their way through.
Oh this battle was fought all in Stanhope town,
When the chimneys did reek and the soot it fell down
Such a battle was ne'er fought in Stanhope before
And I hope such a battle will ne'er be fought more.

And so what of the first Battle of Stanhope .... see Page 62.

10. Quarrying

No book on walking round Stanhope would be complete without mentioning quarrying. This industry has left such visible scars in the landscape that they can't fail to be noticed no matter which direction you walk out of the town.

Quarrying was developed initially to supply the needs of the local area for limestone both to enrich the soil and to meet building needs.

To produce a fertiliser, limestone was first burnt in limekilns to produce quicklime which was then slaked with water to produce hydrated lime, a valuable additive which when spread over fields reduces the acidity of the soil and provides richer grazing for livestock. During the centuries most of the fields in the dale have been treated in this manner particularly as agriculture moved further up the dale and utilised the poorer quality land from the surrounding moors.

For building use limestone was considered "too damp" to be suitable for housing although it was used extensively for wall building and for outbuildings where the need for dryness was not of such importance. However it was as a cement where Weardale lime was in demand throughout the country. The particular variety of lime from Weardale produced a distinctive white lime mortar compared to the more yellow shade. This can be seen in many of the buildings within the dale and helps give them that characteristic Weardale look.

In the early part of the 19th century agricultural improvements throughout the country led to a large upsurge in the need for fertiliser and as a result for limestone. This was followed in the middle of the century by the rapid development of the iron and steel industry where limestone had a further use as a flux in the blast furnaces. Both these factors led to a large increase in the demand resulting in the large scale exploitation of the outcrops of limestone along the sides of the dale. Stanhope became the centre of this industry and its importance resulted in rail links to both Tyneside and Teesside in order to move the rock to both customers and ports.

Demand for limestone reached its peak during the First World War with fifteen quarries being active in the dale. Since this peak, advances in the chemical process of producing hydrated lime and cheaper sources from abroad have resulted in the decline of this once thriving industry. Nowadays the remains are a series of grassed over spoil heaps and the cliffs of the old quarry faces.

WALK 1: CROW COAL HILL

A varied walk that explores the moors that lie to the north west of Stanhope and on the way discovers a hidden rhododendron plantation, prehistoric history and the remains of a coal mining past. The route starts with a woodland walk up through Stanhope Dene before heading across the moors via track to the ridge between Stanhope and Rookhope. The ridgeline is then followed across open moor to the trig point on Crow Coal Hill before descending through the Park back to Stanhope Dene and the return to Stanhope.

DISTANCE: 9.3 mile (14.9 km)
ASCENT: 1,142 feet (348 metres)
TERRAIN: A mixture of woodland path and moorland track coupled with a lengthy stretch across pathless open moor.
TIME: 4.5 to 5.5 hours.
START: Stanhope Market Place. GR NY 996 391.
MAP: OL307 Consett & Derwent Reservoir.
DOGS: Dogs are not allowed on this walk as a sizeable portion of the walk is over access land where they are excluded.
ACCESS: The first half of the route upto the shooting hut is on public rights of way. From there the walk is on access land until it re-enters the woods to finish the walk back to Stanhope on footpaths.
NAVIGATION: Relatively easy following the moorland track although following the pathless ridgeline over Reahope Moor could be tricky and need the use of a compass in poor visibility.

Grid References

Stanhope Market Place	996 391
Road/lane junction	990 393
Stone bridge	985 410
Gate	982 419
Shooting Lodge	963 432
Cairn	954 428
Crow Coal Hill	959 404
Gate	969 404
Track/road junction	982 406
Road/track junction	982 402
Stanhope Market Place	996 391

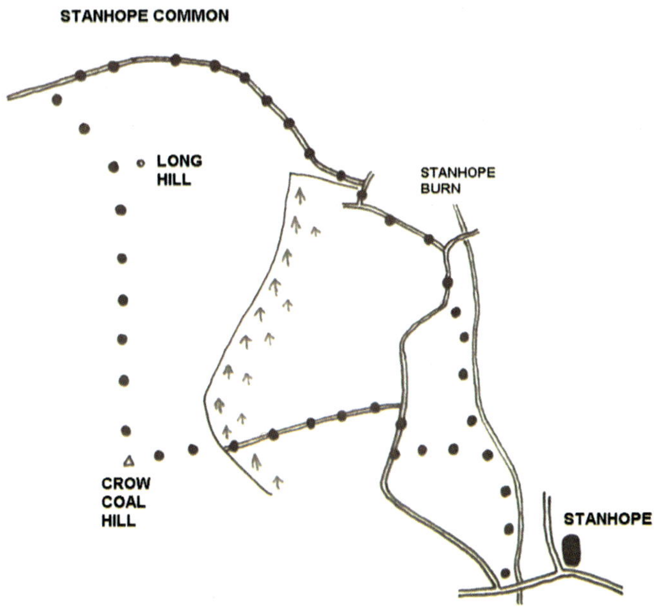

FGS Grading
Grading is F8 [D1, N2, T2, R2, H1]

Distance	**1**	6 – 12 miles
Navigation	**2**	Competent navigation skills needed
Terrain	**2**	25 -50% on graded track or path 50 – 75% off track
Remoteness	**2**	Countryside not in close proximity to habitation – less than 20% of the route within 2 miles
Height	**1**	Over 100 ft per mile

THE WALK.

1. From the Market Place head out of Stanhope on the A689 road going towards Alston. Walk on the footpath on the right side of the road and as you are leaving Stanhope cross the bridge over the Stanhope Burn and here you will find a large road sign and just after it a lane with a footpath sign pointing up it, see photo above. **GR 990 393.**

2. Head up the lane passing a couple of cottages with Stanhope Old Hall looming behind them. Follow the route indicated by the waymarkers, it's all carefully marked along here to stop you ending up in someone's garden. After passing the cottages the path takes you through a small area of open woodland, ignore the footbridge over the Stanhope Burn and stay on the left side of the stream. The path now brings you to a small gate that leads you onto a narrow fenced lane that in turn opens into the wooded slopes of Stanhope Dene.

Stanhope Dene is a very pleasant area consisting of two miles of woodland walks and was laid out on the west side of the town during 1892. At the time conditions for the quarrymen working in the area surrounding Stanhope were pretty grim and despite being non-unionised, in this year they organised a strike for better conditions. Not a decision taken lightly as in those days with no social security, if you didn't work then there was no income and there was the distinct probability of financial hardship for most of the strikers and their families. However the people of Stanhope rallied round and supported the quarrymen financially during the dispute and as a measure of gratitude the strikers laid out the Dene complete with footpaths, seats, bridges, bandstand and a summer house.

The path is relatively easy to follow although it does climb and descend the slopes a number of times. At one point the path does approach a second footbridge but again don't cross, continue on the left bank up and through the woods. Eventually the path leaves the cover of the trees to emerge into an open space and as it does so it also curves away from the Stanhope Burn to find itself rising above the deeply cut gorge of the Reahope Burn. Follow the path as it climbs up above the waterfall to run alongside a wooden fence where it comes to a stile. Cross the stile and then bear right to follow the fence to a gate leading onto a stone bridge spanning the Reahope. **GR 985 410.**

The deeply cut gorge of the Reahope Burn.

3. Go through the gate and follow the walled lane as it makes its way between the buildings of Shield Hurst. The lane starts to descend back towards the valley of the Stanhope Burn but before it gets there a track entrance is meet on the left with a collection of green wheelie bins normally stood alongside. Turn left onto the track and start to head uphill again with an open expanse of fields on the left side and the densely packed woods on the right. As you make your way uphill the buildings of High House come into view but before you reach them the track meets a junction with another track turning right to run under the trees. Take this right turning and after a short distance under the trees come to a gate leading onto the open moor. **GR 982 419.**

4. Go through the gate and ignoring the track going straight on, bear to the left to follow the obvious main track as it heads uphill across the open moor. As you walk away from the woods there are two tracks that leave the main track and head back to the woods, ignore these and stay on the main track. This track is followed all the way to a shooting lodge nestled inside the most remote rhododendron plantation that you'll come across, at least in the Durham Dales. Along the way the track passes one of the old railway wagons that are scattered across the moorland of Durham. It always amazes me some of the places that they appear in. You have no chance of missing the shooting lodge when you arrive at it and the clump of trees and rhododendrons form an oasis in the heather moorland. **GR 963 432.**

Approaching the shooting lodge and its plantation.

5. Follow the track out the other side of the plantation and climb to the ridge between Long Law and Law Hill. As you near the ridge the cairn on the skyline becomes more visible and as you get closer the track bends to the right and at this point a faint path leaves the track and goes straight on towards some grouse butts. Follow this path and just keep going in a straight line to arrive at the cairn. **GR 954 428.**

The cairn is built on top of what is thought to be a Bronze Age burial mound. Look closely at the ground on which it is built and it has the appearance of a small hill built on top of the natural hill. This mound is the northern of three mounds built along the ridge line, two including this one have cairns built on top of them while the middle of the three has a stone sheep fold built on top. Presumably the majority of the stones used in the fold came from the mound

Looking from the cairn on the first mound to the sheep fold on the second.

itself. For more details on these mounds see the section "Prehistoric Stanhope".

6. From this cairn and mound the intention is to walk along the ridge to link all the three mounds together and from there continue along the ridge to Crow Coal Hill. Head south east towards the sheepfold and then the second cairn. The high spot of Long Hill does not lie on the straight line of the ridge but rather to the left of it and here you have a route choice. The first option is to avoid the high ground altogether and keeping to the same height as the cairn, skirt round to the right of the hill and start heading nearly due south to stay on the ridge going over Reahope and Shank. The second choice is to climb the top of Long Hill which is done by just following a straight line from the last cairn upto the highest ground. However care must be taken when leaving the summit so as to not continue going in a straight line which will take you down into the valley and miss the ridge. Instead bear to the right and head due south and the ridge line will open up in front of you.

Continue along the ridge line and what appears to be your first obstacle soon appears in front of you. However the deep gully of Shank Sike is nowhere near as bad as it first appears. Closer inspection shows that it is not as deep nor as boggy as the first impression gives and it is easily crossed. Head up the other side and you'll soon come across a rather interesting little piece of industrial archaeology. On the left of the ridge lies a long channel that has been cut into the ground and it is worth taking time out from the walk to explore this curiosity.

Although dry now, this channel has the appearance of having been built to control a water flow and this is given more credibility when you follow the channel downhill. Built across it is a small stone structure, the appearance suggests that water flowed in one end and out the other. Next to the structure is a large timber with what looks like notch marks cut into it as if it was part of a sluice gate. The hill above the channel is known as East Slate Quarry Hill and there are old quarry and pit workings further down the hill into the valley so presumably there is a connection between one of these and this man-made water course.

The man-made water course and stone ruins.

Return back to the ridgeline and as this starts to descend towards Reahope Moor the trig point on Crow Coal Hill becomes visible in the distance. Head straight for the trig point, there are a couple of quad tracks crossing the col of Reahope Moor and heading up to Crow Coal and these make the walking easier. Arrive at the pock-marked summit of the hill and take a few minutes to explore the lumps and depressions and also take in the views. The trig point makes a good vantage point and Stanhope itself is clearly visible. **GR 959 404.**

7. From the trig point turn left to head downhill towards the woods at the bottom of the hill. You are making for a gate in the wall surrounding the woods but you are unlikely to hit it exactly so just head downhill on a bearing of 80 degrees which will take you to the left of the gate and then when you come to the

Looking from the trig point towards Stanhope.

perimeter wall bear right to follow it until you arrive at the gate, see photo below. **GR 969 404.**

The gate leading in to the woods.

8. Go through the gate into the woods and past the sheep pens. When I first walked this route the farmer was marking his sheep here and they were all penned in-between the gates at either end of the wood. It was the first time in walking that I literally had to force my way through a flock of sheep. When exiting the woods you are confronted by two gates, go through the left hand one and follow the track past the buildings of Mount Pleasant, keeping the wall on your right side. Follow the track downhill past the farm of Pease Mires where another track comes in on the left and arrive at the roadside. **GR 982 406.**

9. Turn right onto the road and follow it past Keeper's Lodge until you come to the entrance of the farm of Widley Field on the left of the road. The track giving access to the farm is also the first footpath encountered on that side of the road and there is the usual footpath sign as you leave the road. **GR 982 402.**

Heading down to Widleyfield.

10. Go down the track and past the right side of the house. Behind the building is a gate into the field that is impossible to open and so you just have to scramble over it. Once past the gate walk to the end of the field and then follow the bottom fence to the left where you will find a small gate leading back into the wooded Stanhope Dene where you walked up several hours ago. Go through the gate and turn right onto the path to retrace those early steps back to Stanhope. When you arrive back at the road turn left to come back to the Market Place.

CROW COAL HILL

Names often tell a story in themselves and though the name Crow Coal may sound a little peculiar it does actually give part of the history of this hill.

Crow coal is the name given to a poor quality grade of coal. Not having the fiery heat needed for industrial use this coal was mostly used for domestic heating where it could lay slowly smouldering away on the hearth. It was also sometimes used in lime kilns which may have been the case here as Weardale enjoyed a prolonged period of field improvement during the 17th and 18th centuries.

Not being valuable enough to justify the expense of deep shafts, crow coal was normally extracted from seams that were relatively close to the surface quite often using what were called bell pits. As you approach the trig point on Crow Coal Hill you'll notice the ground around the summit is pock-marked with dips and depressions giving a dimpled effect to the ground. These probably represent the remains of a series of bell pits used to extract the coal from which the hill derives its name.

Bell pits date back to mediaeval times although they were also used much later. The pit consisted of a simple shaft dug down to the coal seam which lay close to

Depressions left from the old bell shaft workings around the summit trig point.

the surface. As the seam was worked a chamber was opened out giving the appearance of a bell-shape hence the name. When one working was finished, it was then filled in with the debris and rubble from the new pit that was being dug.

The workings of a bell pit above and the sunken depressions left behind once filled in after the seam was exhausted.

WALK 2: COLLIER LAW AND THE STANHOPE BURN

A high moorland walk that follows paths and tracks to the summit of Collier Law before descending down across pathless moor ,complete with some tussock jumping and bog hopping, to Parkhead Station. From the Station a descent is made into the valley of the Stanhope Burn which is then followed as it cuts its way downstream through the bedrock of the moor to the wooded slopes of its lower valley. A woodland walk between the trees on these slopes brings you back to Stanhope.

DISTANCE: 9.0 mile (14.5 km)
ASCENT: 1,201 feet (366 metres)
TERRAIN: Most of the route over the moor is on path or track although there is a sizeable portion over tussocky open moor complete with boggy bits to get your feet wet. The path following the Stanhope Burn is eroded in places and does have a few steep drops beside it but should not present any problems to the average walker. Towards the bottom of the valley a point is reached where it would be advisable to stay low and close to the stream.
The burn itself is crossed twice while making your way down the valley which in times of bad weather could prove hazardous.
TIME: 4.5 to 5.5 hours.
START: Stanhope Market Place. GR NY 996 391.
MAP: OL307 Consett & Derwent Reservoir.
DOGS: Not allowed on the access land.
ACCESS: A mix of rights of way and access land.
REFRESHMENTS ON ROUTE: Parkhead Station, a cafe stop on the Coast to Coast Cycle Way.

Grid References

Stanhope Market Place	996 391
Gate	996 399
Track/railway junction	994 407
Railway/track junction	996 414
Collier Law	016 418
Parkhead Station	003 431
Wilkinson's Cut	996 437
Bridge	986 414
Stanhope Market Place	996 391

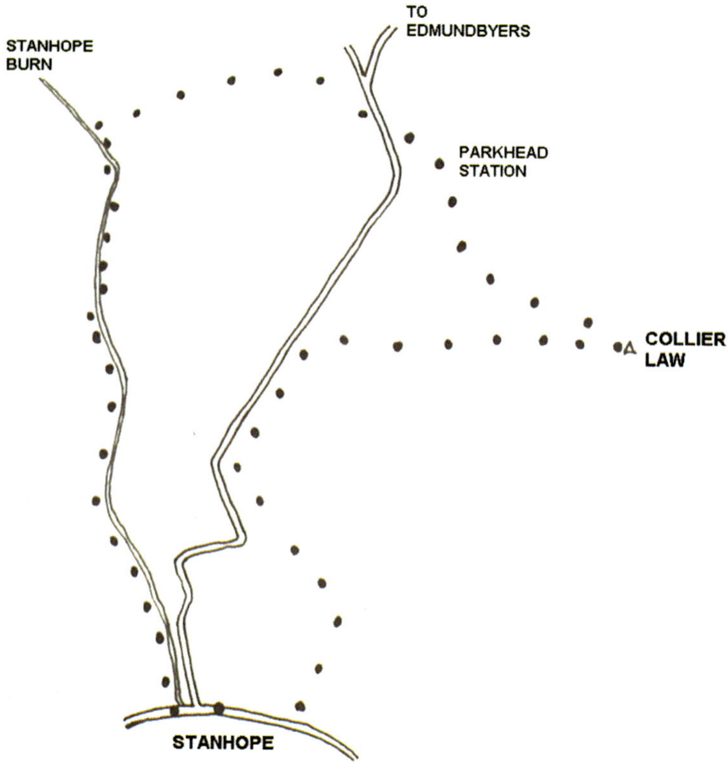

FGS Grading

Grading is F9 [D1, N2, T2, R2, H2]

Distance	**1**	6 – 12 miles
Navigation	**2**	Competent navigation skills needed
Terrain	**2**	25 -50% on graded track or path 50 – 75% off track
Remoteness	**2**	Countryside not in close proximity to habitation – less than 20% of the route within 2 miles
Height	**2**	Over 125 ft per mile

THE WALK.

1. From the Market Place head up the lane in-between the church and The Bonny Moorhen pub, see photo above. At the top of the lane turn left to walk down the road and just after Stanhope Methodist Church take the footpath on the right leading up between the buildings towards the moors. Go through the small gate and follow the path straight on over a crossroads before crossing two bridges spanning the old quarry workings. Go through another small gate and then follow the fence as it bears left to run above the quarries. This is a nice green path running alongside the fence but shortly you'll spy a cottage on the slopes above and another path that leaves the fence and heads up towards a gate in the wall leading to the cottage. Climb up to the gate, see photo over page.
GR 996 399.

2. Go through the gate and also the second gate next to it to get onto the moor. Turn left and follow the path as it heads up the side of the hill. As you reach the lip of the hill a path comes in from the right, it is hard to decide whether this path is joining you or you are joining it, but keep going in the same direction. As you walk along you'll find two paths heading off to the left, the second one being close to some ruins and has a prominent waymarker that could confuse. However stay on the current path as it curves round and heads towards the walls that surround the buildings of the old Crawley Engine site, ***see The Moorland Railways***. Follow the wall around the buildings to come onto a track where you bear left and that after a hundred yards or so will bring you to the bottom of a disused railway line, just before you come to the main B6278 road.
GR 994 407.

The path leaving the fence line and heading up to the gate in the wall just before the cottage.

3. Turn right and follow the rail track uphill passing the disused Crawley Reservoir as you do. After 1/2 mile a walled enclosure appears on the left side of the track bed and as the enclosure ends a vehicle track cuts across the old rail line and heads up Bashaw Rigg. **GR 996 414.**

The track leading off from the track-bed and heading upto Bashaw Rigg.

4. Turn right onto the vehicle track and follow as it climbs up the moor. Eventually the track comes into view of an old sandstone quarry on Millstone Rigg where the track joins onto a hard surfaced dirt road that serves the radio mast on Collier Law. Turn right onto the road and follow it until you come to the buildings and radio mast. On the way pass a second smaller transmitter mast, you wouldn't get confused as to which is the right one. When you arrive at the main mast leave the track and head round the right side of the buildings to find the trig point behind them and on the other side of the watershed fence.
GR 016 418.

5. At the trig point bear left to follow the fence. There is a small path running alongside the fence but the terrain is rough and tussocky and the path is very easy to lose. Initially the ground is a bit wet and boggy as you make your way over West Collierlaw Moss and at times you will have to make a diversion away from the fence to avoid pools, some of which can be quite deep. As you leave the moss the ground becomes firmer and it becomes easier to stay close to the fence. After a bend in the fence you come to another disused quarry which reaches quite close to the fence line and you do have to stay near to the fence at this point but there is no danger and it is soon passed. The ground on the other side of the fence becomes a bit of a waste ground now, this area has been extensively quarried for sand and the result is something akin to desolation. Keep following the fence and as you descend the buildings at Parkhead Station start to come into view which is where you are now making for. As you get nearer to

Approaching Parkhead Station.

the buildings it is possible to leave the fence and cut the corner to head straight to them. The old railway track that you initially started to follow back at Crawley Engine has now made its way up the moor and now meets you at the station where it continues onwards as the Waskerley Way.
Parkhead Station GR 003 431.

6. Bear left in front of the station to follow the access track to the main road. Cross the road and head up the embankment as indicated by the footpath signs and follow the path along the old railway line. This path is part of the Coast to Coast Cycle Way so there is a probability that you might meet a mountain bike or two. After about 1/2 mile the path comes to Wilkinson's Cut where the path mounts the embankment on the left while the bed of the old trackway continues along the level boggy ground. Mount the embankment and then bear left, **GR 996 437**, to head downhill into the valley. See photo below.

Approaching Wilkinson's Cut with the path going up the embankment on the left before heading down into the valley.

7. Head downhill and after passing under the power lines a faint vehicle/quad track will start to come into view. Follow this down the slope until you come to the edge of the Stanhope Burn valley where the track bears to the right and descends steeply to meet the burn at the point where the West Whiteley Burn flows into it. Turn left and follow the bank downstream. At times the path gets a little bit narrow and rises up above the burn and a little bit of care needs to be taken on these places.

Walking alongside the Stanhope Burn.

After 1/4 of a mile the path approaches a flat area of stream bank and some strange shapes will start to greet you. Quite a number of "stone men" have been erected here, rocks placed on top of each other with some of them reaching above waist height. Presumably built by people coming up from Stanhope, judging by the size of the stones some of these will have taken a considerable

The stone men beside the burn.

effort to move into location. I hope that they stay in place as they add a bit of "other worldish" charm to this section of the burn.

Stay following the path and shortly after passing the stone men two buildings are approached. At this point a track comes down one side of the valley, crosses the burn via a ford and then goes back up the other side. Use the ford to cross the burn, there is a steep slope on the left bank here and for a short distance the right bank is followed. Ignore the vehicle track as it climbs up the hillside and instead continue straight on following the burn and passing an old sheep fold as you do.

The steep slope on the left bank is clearly visible and once past it make your way back to the burn and cross back over as soon as possible. Continue following the path down the left bank and after 1/2 mile a wall comes down to the water's edge on the right side of the burn and on the left side your path branches into two. Try and stay low and close to the burn. The higher path is badly eroded and a bit hairy to negotiate so it is not recommended. Keep following the burn to come to a bridge with a collection of sheep pens next to it. Next to the pens a couple of red metal hurdles act as a gate through the fence onto the road. **GR 986 414.**

8. Turn right onto the road to cross the bridge and start heading uphill. Ignore the turning on the right with its collection of green wheelie bins and continue along the lane passing between the buildings at the farm of Shield Hurst. Shortly after this you'll cross a bridge over the Reahope Burn and at the far end of the bridge come to a closed gate. If you've done these walks in the order that they are set out in this book then you'll have probably recognised Shield Hurst and this stretch of the route as we came out this way when leaving Stanhope on the Crow Coal Hill walk. Go through the gate and turn left to find a stile in the fence, cross and find yourself above the gorge that the Reahope Burn has carved out of the rocks. Follow this path as it makes its way down through the wooded Stanhope Dene. Remember to ignore the two footbridges that you pass and stay on the right bank of Stanhope Burn. As you'll know from the start of the Crow Coal Hill walk the path through the dene comes out on the A689 road as it leaves Stanhope and here turn left to walk along the road back to the Market Place.

As you will have noticed from the Crow Coal Hill walk the valley of the Stanhope Burn is a peaceful, tranquil place but in the 1800's it fairly quaked with the noise of industry. Surprisingly this small valley was an important site of lead mining, smelting, iron working and limestone quarrying. The Ordnance Survey map of 1861 shows that within Stanhopeburn, note the subtle differ-

ence in name, there lay five quarries, at least five lead mines, a crushing mill, a washing floor, a lead smelting mill, a blast furnace for processing iron ore and the terminus of the Stanhope and Tyne Railway. And this is all in the 2 1/2 miles from the sheep pens down to Stanhope.

The vast bulk of this industry was on the left bank of the burn as you head downstream. For those with an interest in industrial archaeology it is possible to stay on the left bank by following the tarmac road from the sheep pens down through the old workings until you come to the B6278 road above Crawleyside. The route described above follows the right bank down through the woods, it's a much prettier route.

THE MOORLAND RAILWAYS

Due to the extraction of minerals, limestone and iron ore Weardale was generating great wealth during the 19th century. However transportation in the dale was very much in need of improvement and the need to move large quantities of limestone and iron ore was the driving force behind the introduction of the railway.

The most ambitious of these projects was the Stanhope and Tyne Railway which was intended to link the quarries of Weardale with the ironworks of Consett and then ultimately the ports on the River Tyne. Crawleyside was to be the starting point in Stanhope due to its proximity to the limestone quarries at Lanehead in Stanhope Burn and the line would run up the slope of Crawleyside and then over the moors of Stanhope Common, Waskerley Park and Muggleswick Common before eventually reaching the Tyne at South Shields. Robert Stephenson was appointed consultant engineer and the line was to be the highest standard gauge railway in England.

Construction started at Stanhope in July 1832 and the line was officially opened in 1834. The line itself was a marvel of engineering with at least sixteen inclines included within its construction, the first being right from the start up the steep bank of Crawleyside. Here the line used a 50 horse power stationary steam engine to haul the laden wagons up on ropes from the terminus in Lanehead Quarry to Crawley Engine, a journey where the main gradient was an extremely steep 1 in 8 and where there was an additional complication of having to pass through a tunnel that took the line under the B6278 road.

Part of the cutting leading to the tunnel under the B6278.

Once at Crawley Engine the ropes were then changed to hook the wagons to another stationary steam engine and they were then towed upto Weatherhill Engine a route that itself had gradients of 1 in 13. By the use of this ingenious system wagons fully laden with limestone were able to be moved over a vertical height of 650 feet in just over 1 1/2 miles. Horses where then used to pull the wagons to Parkhead and from then on a combination of horses and self-acting inclines took the wagons to Consett and South Shields.

In 1845 a branch line was started from a junction constructed at Parkhead, now known as Parkhead Station, that ran round the head of Stanhope Burn and went to the quarries of Rookhope. This opened the following year in 1846.

Despite financial difficulties, mergers, buy-outs and nationalisation the line lasted in its entirety until 1951 when the Crawleyside Incline was closed. The original stationary engines at both the Crawley and Weatherhill Inclines being still in operation till 1918, a sound testament to their construction. After the closure of the Incline the remainder of the line from Weatherhill to Consett was still in operation until 1968 and was used to move sand that was excavated from the Weatherhill quarry.

Nowadays the track bed above Crawley Engine is used as a walkway and the branch line from Parkhead to Rookhope is part of the popular Coast to Coast cycle way. Sections of the old rail line and the branch line to Rookhope are used on both the Collier Law and the Stanhope Burn walk and the Rookhope Circular route while the remains of the tunnel under the B6278 that the Crawleyside Incline passed through can be seen on the A Walk Round The Park route.

Looking back down the old rail bed towards Crawley Engine.

WALK 3: CARRS TOP

An exceptional walk dominated by the views from the trig point on Carrs Top. On a warm sunny day with good visibility this hill can give some of the best views in the Durham Dales. Although not particularly high, the positioning and surrounding landforms of ridges and valleys show Weardale, the Bollihope valley and even the farthest reaches of the Wear valley as the exceptional countryside that it is.

On the day that I test-walked this route the views were given an added lustre by watching a pair of red kites soaring above the valleys. The lunch break taken at the summit of Carrs Top was extended by twenty minutes as a result. What could be better than sitting with your back against a trig point on a warm, sunny day drinking tea and watching these large elegant birds of prey soaring effortlessly high over Weardale and then Bollihope before drifting off in the direction of Teesdale.

The red kites seen are a pair of the birds re-introduced as part of the Northern Kites program. Released in the Gateshead area a male and female have found their way down to the reaches of upper Teesdale and have taken residence between Eggleston and Langleydale. Hopefully in time they will breed successfully and sightings of this majestic bird will become more common place.

DISTANCE: 9.9 miles (15.8 km)
ASCENT: 1,634 feet (498 metres)
TERRAIN: The walk does start with field paths followed by a road walk to gain access to the moor. Once on the moor it is relatively pathless walking upto and down from the trig point on Carrs Top although there are one or two quad tracks that ease the walking slightly. The second half of the walk does follow tracks up and over the ridge line of Catterick before descending on field paths back to Stanhope.
TIME: 5 to 6 hours.
START: Stanhope Market Place. GR NY 996 391.
MAP: OL31 North Pennines Teesdale and Weardale.
DOGS: Not allowed on the access land.
ACCESS: The majority of this walk is on public access land although rights of way are used to gain access to and from the moor.

Grid References

Stanhope Market Place	996 391
Track/road junction	989 386
Footpath sign	986 372
Carrs Top	961 355
Quad track	968 346
Road	985 352
Parking area	988 351
Track junction	998 354
Gate	002 364
Road	001 382
Stile	002 383
Stanhope Market Place	996 391

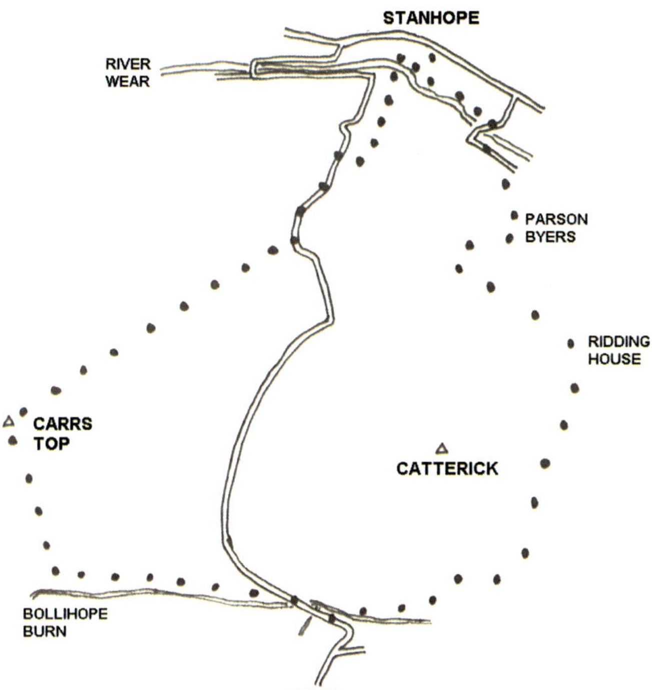

FGS Grading

Grading is F9 [D1, N2, T2, R2, H2]

Distance	**1**	6 – 12 miles
Navigation	**2**	Competent navigation skills needed
Terrain	**2**	25 -50% on graded track or path 50 – 75% off / single track
Remoteness	**2**	Countryside not in close proximity to habitation – less than 20% of the route within 2 miles
Height	**2**	Over 125 ft per mile

The start from the Market Place, heading down The Butts and going towards the riverside.

THE WALK.

1. From the Market Place head down the Butts in front of the Pack Horse Inn and follow it to the riverside where a tarmac path runs along the bank, see photo on previous page. Follow the path upstream to a footbridge over the River Wear and cross, then turn right to follow the track on the other side. Leave the track and go through the gate marked "Private" that leads into the sports ground of Unthank Park. See photo. Despite the sign this is a public right of way so there will be no problem on access.

The entrance to Unthank Park.

Pass in front of the pavilion and head towards the ladder stile in front of you to cross the railway line. Once across the line head across the field to the 11 o'clock position to find a gated stile to the right of the tree. Cross the stile and follow the wall uphill to pass through another gated stile. As you continue up through the next field a bank hides the fence and track from view until you are right on top of it. Cross the fence onto the track and then turn right to follow the track to the B6278 road. **GR 989 386.**

2. Turn left onto the road to follow it uphill. This next stretch follows the road up to the open moor and sounds a bit dull but is actually not as bad as it first seems as the views are quite good and provide some consolation. Follow the road past the huge Newlandside Quarry until you come to a cattle grid. At this point the wall on the left does a 90 degree turn to head away from the road but the wall on the right stays with the road even though it moves away a bit. Continue following the road until the wall on the right finally decides to depart and here there is a bend in the road with a footpath sign on the right side **GR 986 372.**

Leaving the road at the footpath sign and heading for the high ground.

3. Leave the road at the footpath sign but ignore the direction indicated by the sign and instead continue straight on heading for the highest point on the horizon. The route eventually crosses a quad track and here you have a route choice, you can continue going straight on heading for the high spot or you can turn right to follow the quad track which follows a sweeping curve to come back and rejoin the straight line option. Going straight ahead is rougher walking than the quad track but the quad track is longer, the choice is yours. If you follow the straight line option then when the quad track comes back and rejoins the route, follow it as it now makes its way towards the summit of Carrs Top. A few hundred metres further on and a small stream is crossed and shortly after that the track separates into two with both tracks going either side of the summit. Stay on the right hand track and soon this will start to curve through the boulder field or Carrs that give the hill its name. The route goes below and to the right of the cairn at the end of the summit plateau. Follow the track onto the plateau and find the trig point straight ahead. **GR 961 355.**

Having a break on Carrs Top.

4. Leave the trig point by turning left and heading straight down into the Bollihope Valley. As you head downhill you'll cross a quad track before passing to the left of a sheep fold and then as you reach the lip of the valley you'll meet a second quad track that is running along the valley edge. **GR 968 346.**

5. Turn left to follow the quad track and as you make your way along it the track moves away from both the valley edge and the Bollihope Burn. The track is relatively easy to follow and makes its way past an old tin shed and later on a pair of sheepfolds. Eventually you arrive at a large walled enclosure called Peg's House, which due to its position alongside the Roman road that lies under the B6278 has long been speculated as being the remains of a Romano-British settlement. Follow clockwise round the outside of the walls before descending to meet the roadside. **GR 985 352.**

6. Turn right onto the road and follow it over the Bollihope Burn and then across a second bridge over its tributary, the Harnisha Burn. After this second bridge there is a level space on the left hand side of the road that used to be a car parking area. **GR 988 351.**

7. Leave the road and cross over the bank and ditch that now prevents vehicle access and bear to the right to head for the corner of the wooded area on the

The old parking area, leave the road and head for the corner of the trees.

other side of the burn. See photo above. Cross the stream using the ford that is next to these trees and then follow the track uphill. The track gets quite steep in places as it makes its way through an area of old quarry workings but does level out once it starts to wind its way along the shoulder of Catterick. You do pass a couple of faint side tracks but just over 1/2 mile after splodging across the ford you come to a junction with a track going off to the left that heads up and over the Catterick ridgeline. **GR 998 354.**

8. Turn left onto this track and follow it over and down the other side of the hill. As you come to the bottom of the moor a wall comes in from the left to form a corner and at this point the track does a sharp turn to the right. Leave the track here to go straight on following the wall downhill to join the Weardale Way where it goes through a small gate in the wall corner. **GR 002 364.**

9. For the next couple of miles the route follows the Weardale Way so go through the gate and follow the left hand wall down through the field. At the bottom of the field go through the stile next to the gate with the Weardale Way marker pointing straight on. This will bring you out on a crossroads and here you go straight on through the gate in front even though this has no marker on. One word of caution, when the walk was tested this gate was tied tightly shut and had to be climbed. Once through the gate head towards the farm of Ridding

The track heading down from the Catterick ridge.

House that you could see over the rise of the hill and pick up a track which goes to an open gateway to the left of the building.

Go through the gateway and immediately turn left to follow a trackway to the end of the field. Go through the gate and continue following the track. This soon disappears in the field being replaced by a number of paths and sheep trods. As you walk, slowly bear to the right making your way to the fence that runs along the edge of the quarry.

Follow the fence line to the point where you descend to cross a dry stream bed and once across climb the steep bank and as you do so follow the wall in front as it bears to the left to come to a gap between the wall and a fenced enclosure that surrounds what appears to be an old shaft. Go through the gap to arrive at a gate in the right hand wall, pass through the gate and cut through the field heading towards the fence opposite which again runs along the top of the quarry. Follow the fence round the quarry's edge and a track materialises which is followed through some old workings. At one point the track gets a bit difficult to identify but follow a line of trees to arrive at a gate. Go through the gate and turn left onto the track on the other side and this will slowly descend to a crossroads.

Go straight over the crossroads to come to the buildings of Parson Byers where

The old quarry after Ridding House.

the track takes a sharp turn to the right. At this point there is a very prominent footpath marker pointing over the fields but ignore this and continue on the track as it passes on the left of the buildings. Just past the last building the wall on the left has a gate and stile proudly carrying the Weardale Way marker, go over the stile and follow the obvious diagonal path across the field heading towards the row of houses on the road below. Cross the stile opposite the houses to join the road. **GR 001 382.**

10. Turn left and follow the road. When you come to the entrance to the Heather View Holiday Park, the Weardale Way continues straight on through the park but this is where you leave it to follow the road as it bends right to cross the two bridges over the railway and the river. Shortly after the second bridge come to a footpath sign on the left side of the road with a stile in the wall. **GR 002 383.**

11. Cross the stile and follow the obvious path to a crossing point over the railway. Once past the railway you'll enter a playing field and here head straight across the field making for the metal gate behind the goal posts. Follow this path and it will cross the rail line again before coming out at the bottom of the Butts where you started the walk. Turn right onto the road and follow it back up to the Market Place.

WALK 4: FATHERLEY HILL

A walk that climbs the hills to the east of Stanhope and follows the ridgeline between Stanhope and Wolsingham. Although not particularly high in relation to the hills further up the dale, these hills and in particular Fatherley Hill with its currick on top can give excellent views out over Weardale and the wide expanse of moorland that surrounds Stanhope.

DISTANCE: 6.3 mile (10.1 km)
ASCENT: 1,178 feet (359 metres)
TERRAIN: The start of the walk is over field paths that lead to the open moor and this includes a fairly steep descent down some awkward steps to cross the footbridge over the Shittlehope Burn. Once on the open moor, quad bike and vehicle tracks are followed although no moorland walk would be complete without a soft, squishy bit and this one is no exception and the final pull up to Collier Law leaves the quad track to follow a well-defined but boggy path through heather and peat.
TIME: 4 to 5 hours.
START: Stanhope Market Place. GR NY 996 391.
MAP: OL307 Consett & Derwent Reservoir.
DOGS: The bulk of this route is on access land and dogs are not allowed.
ACCESS: Apart from the field paths that allow access both on and off the moor virtually all of the remainder of the route is over access land.

Grid References

Stanhope Market Place	996 391
Road/footpath junction	001 393
Stile in wall	009 389
Track crossroads	010 389
Fence and gate	023 388
Fence and gate	017 417
Gate onto road	004 395
Stanhope Market Place	996 391

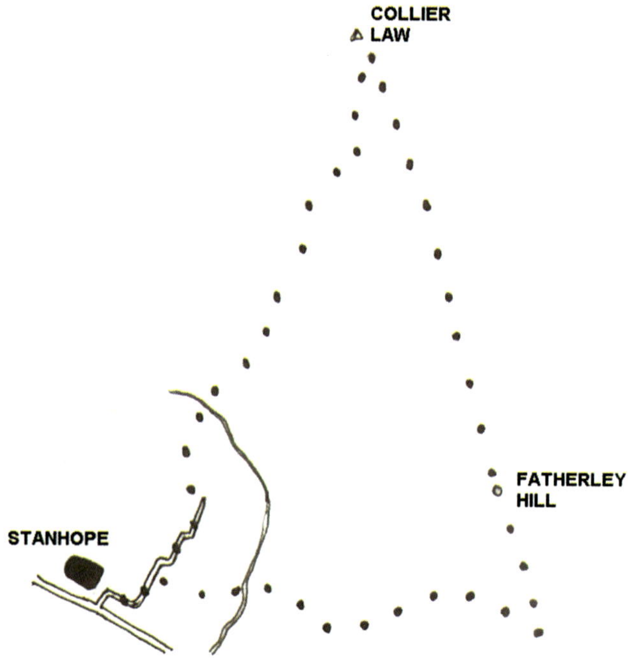

FGS Grading
Grading is F7 [D1, N1, T1, R2, H2]

Distance	**1**	6 – 12 miles
Navigation	**1**	Basic navigation skills needed
Terrain	**1**	50 – 75% on graded track or path 25 – 50% off track
Remoteness	**2**	Countryside not in close proximity to habitation – less than 20% of the route within 2 miles
Height	**2**	Over 125 ft per mile

THE WALK.

1. From the market place head up the lane between the church and the Bonny Moorhen pub, see the photo on page 27 . At the top of the lane turn right and follow the road past two turnings on the right and where the third road comes in on the right bear left to follow it steeply uphill until you come to a footpath sign on the right side of the road and a stile in the wall. See photo below.
GR 001 393.

The stile crossing the wall to start the walk across the fields.

2. Cross the stile to enter the field and then follow the fence and in front of you will appear two gates. Head to the left hand gate and you'll find the first of a series of newly constructed wooden kissing gates. Pass through and continue following the wall to pass through a second and then a third gate. After passing through the third gate the wall on the right has disappeared and you are faced with an open field. Instead of taking the obvious route straight ahead to the gate opposite, bear to the left towards the corner of the field to find another one of the new kissing gates. Pass through and straight in front see a stile over a wire fence that runs along the top of the valley of the Shittlehope Burn. Cross the stile and descend the steep path down to the footbridge that spans the burn.

From the bridge you are reputably able to see a series of small caves in the rocks that line the steep gorge. These are the Fairy Holes, the caves where the

fairies live. Never been able to see them myself, neither the caves or the fairies.

Cross the bridge and climb the other side and where the path branches take the left hand fork to leave the valley. Cross the stile over the wire fence and head towards the wall on the right where there is a gap and a waymarker post.

There is a nice boggy bit of ground on the other side of the gap but once past that head in the direction indicated by the waymarker, going to the left of the trees and between the two ruins, see photo below, where the path climbs a small rise and arrives at a stile in the wall on the left of an old barn. **GR 009 389.**

Head to the left of the trees and then between the ruins.

3. The stile gives access to the open moor and once across turn left to follow the path as it heads uphill. As the path reaches the lip of the climb it forms a crossroads with another faint path that is running along the edge of the escarpment. Go straight on and in a short distance you will meet a vehicle track, turn right to follow this track.

As you walk along keep your eyes open for small earthworks running alongside the track and in some cases the track cuts through them. Standing only about a foot or so high these are the remains of field boundaries that date back to the prehistoric, possibly the Bronze Age. Sounds strange but four thousand years ago when the climate was milder this moorland was capable of providing good farmland that sustained a substantial and wealthy population.

Keep following the track until you come to a crossroads formed by another track

One of the small earthworks scattered over the moor that mark out prehistoric field boundaries.

coming up from the farm below you and heading up to the top of the moor. **GR 010 389.**

4. At the crossroads turn left to head uphill but before you do look to the right and you'll see the entire route that you have followed up to this point, laid out in front of you all the way back to Stanhope. Follow the track uphill and continue straight on when it is cut by another track running across the slope of the moor. The further you climb you'll notice a wall coming in from the right and the track climbs to meet it and at this point it joins onto a more substantial track that is following the line of the wall. Bear to the left to follow this good track along the side of the wall until it meets a fence and gate. **GR 023 388.**

5. Go through the gate and here we have a route choice. You can either turn left immediately and follow the fence line for a short distance over rough ground until the track comes in to run alongside the fence. Alternatively after going through the gate you could continue on the main track for a short distance and then turn left onto the track that heads back to the fence.

This track follows the fence for quite a while passing the rather impressive currick atop Fatherley Hill. After crossing over the top of Fatherley the fence and track descend with another shooter's track bearing off to the right. Continue following the track running alongside the fence as it starts to climb upwards towards Collier Law and its distinctive radio mast. As it climbs the track ceases

The currack on Fatherley Hill.

to be well-surfaced and goes through a gate leading to the left side of the fence. However stay on the right side of the fence following a path that continues over some boggy ground upto the summit where it joins a vehicle track that has just come through the fence via a gate. **GR 017 417.**

6. Turn left and go through the gate. The trig point marking the top of the hill is hidden behind the buildings of the radio mast. However it is worth going the extra couple of feet upto the fence junction that lies alongside the summit. The views here give an excellent 360 degree panorama and the stone cairn lying at the fence junction is built on what is probably another Bronze Age burial mound.

Retrace your steps back to the track and shortly you will have a newly built dolomite track leading off to the left. Easy to spot, it's big, it's bright and it's yellow. Head off down this yellow brick road back towards Stanhope. At times the gradient is quite steep and you'll question how even a land-rover can make it up here. Praises to the guy who invented first gear.

The yellow track is followed all the way down eventually running alongside the Black Burn until it joins with the Crawley Burn. At this point the track climbs out of the burn valley and makes a sharp right hand turn to pass in front of a green hut.

Stay on the main track as you pass two tracks leading off to the right and then pass the long gouge that is Rogerwell Hush, a stark reminder of the area's mining past. Continue on the track bearing left at the next junction down towards the buildings at Hill Crest where you will pass through a gate onto a tarmac

The track leading away from Fatherley Hill towards the radio mast on Collier Law.

road. **GR 004 395.**

7. Turn right and follow the road downhill. This is the same road that you followed at the start of your walk several hours ago and soon you will pass the point where you turned off to start the walk over the fields towards Shittlehope. Continue on the road retracing your steps or alternatively just head down to the main road where you can turn right and follow the main street back to the Market Place and a rest.

Rogerwell Hush carving an ugly groove in the ground.

WALK 5: EASTGATE CIRCULAR

A shorter and more of a lower level walk through the fields along the side of the valley to Eastgate and back along the banks of the River Wear. For those who want to add on an extra couple of miles there is the option of adding in an additional loop following the path alongside the Rookhope Burn as it heads upstream before returning back to Eastgate via a short road walk to recommence the original route.

DISTANCE: 5.9 mile (9.5 km) Shorter version, 8.1 mile (13 km) Longer version
ASCENT: 371 feet (113 metres) Shorter version, 568 feet (173 metres) Longer version
TERRAIN: The majority of this walk is on field paths some of which is over rough pasture. On the optional longer loop, as the path follows the Rookhope Burn it passes through a couple of small stretches of woodland and at several points the path has suffered erosion and although presenting no real problem may need a little bit of care. There is a road walk of about one and a half miles on this longer loop as the route returns back to Eastgate.
TIME: 3.5 to 4.5 hours Shorter version, 4.5 to 5.5 hours Longer version.
START: Stanhope Market Place. GR NY 996 391.
MAP: OL307 Consett & Derwent Reservoir.
DOGS: Obviously allowed on the rights of way but keep them on a lead. If you do the top loop of the walk there is a lengthy stretch along a country road where traffic could potentially be expected. Narrow wall stiles are throughout this route and these may require you to lift your dog over. Cattle and sheep will be encountered throughout the route. The farmyard at Eastgate House is passed through and you may expect to meet other dogs here. On both loops of the walk you will also pass through caravan sites.
ACCESS: This walk is all on public rights of way.
REFRESHMENTS ON ROUTE: The Cross Keys in Eastgate.

Grid References

Stanhope Market Place	996 391
Road junction	983 394
Thrush Nest	965 392
Eastgate	953 389

Longer route

Path/road junction	945 405
Road junction	952 387

Return route

Caravan site entrance	957 385
Stanhope Market Place	996 391

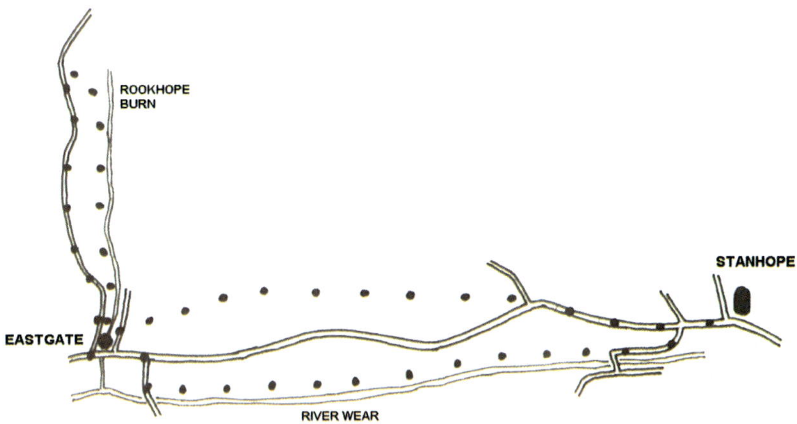

FGS Grading

With there being two possible routes on this walk you do end up with two gradings however the difference is only due to the distance with the short route coming in at T3 [D0, N1, T0, R1, H1] and the longer route at T4 [D1, N1, T0, R1, H1]. The table for the longer route is shown below.

Distance	1	6 – 12 miles
Navigation	1	Basic navigation skills needed
Terrain	1	50 – 75% on graded track or path 25 – 50% off track
Remoteness	1	Countryside in fairly close proximity to habitation – at least 80% of the route within 2 miles
Height	0	Less than 100 ft per mile

THE WALK.

1. From the Market Place leave Stanhope following the A689 to Alston. Walk on the right side of the road as there is footpath all the way. Go past the road junction where the B6278 goes off to the left and a smaller unclassified road goes off to the right. Continue following the A689 and 1/2 mile after leaving Stanhope and just past the sign for the Greenfoot Holiday Park there is a second unclassified road going off to the right, there is a blue cycle route sign for Rookhope pointing up it, see photo on page 66. **GR 983 394.**

2. Instead of turning right up the side road go straight ahead through the layby to find a footpath sign and a gate. Occasionally this layby is used to store materials for road repairs so you may have to negotiate mounds of chippings or other such obstacles. Go through the gate and then follow the fence on the left going straight on through the next two fields. See photo below.

Following the fence line through the fields.

At the end of the second field there is a gated stile into the third but take care as you cross as there is a small stream on the other side with a little bit of a drop down into it. Again follow the fence on the left as you head across the third field but as you get towards the wall at the far end head towards the visible gap lying between the wall and the hedgerow to pass through it. Go across the fourth field keeping the wall on the left to come to another gated stile set in the wall on the opposite side. Cross the stile into an open field and look to the 2 o'clock position to see a gate in the far wall. Head towards it and pass through to find yourself in a small narrow field with walls on both sides. Head towards the buildings where there is a gate in the right hand wall. See photo below. Go through the gate and then straight on between the buildings of Guy's Close to come to a track on the other side of the house.

Approaching Guy's Close. The gate is in the wall on the right in front of the buildings.

Turn left and follow the track to a gate, pass through and keeping the wall on the right head for the next gate straight in front of you. Pass through that and head straight on passing to the right of a metal building and above the house on the slopes just below. Go through the next gate and the buildings of Sweet Wells can be seen in front, head to the 2 o'clock position making for the opposite side of the field and at the point where the fence changes to a wall find a set of stone steps built into the wall. You have to look closely as they are easy to miss.

Climb over the wall and the small stream in the shallow gully that is on the other side and then go straight ahead following an obvious edge to the side of the hill. As you follow the edge, a line of trees and a fence appear on your left and the ruins of the delightfully named Thrush Nest can be seen straight in front. Thrush Nest is one of a number of derelict farms throughout the dale. The post-war decline in farming prices after the end of World War 1 saw many of the smaller farms become bankrupt and their buildings fall into ruins. Continue on to the ruins and when you get there a stile can be found on the left just in front of the buildings where the fence and the wall meet. **GR 965 392.**

Passing in front of the ruins of Thrush Nest.

3. Cross the stile and keeping to the left of the building find a track that descends down the hill. Turn left and follow the track downhill until it comes to a tarmac lane that comes up from the valley floor heading to a disused quarry on the slopes above. Turn right to follow the lane up a small rise and round a corner to find a gate across the lane preventing any further access. At this point bear left to follow the fence going past an open gateway and at the end of the fence where it turns sharply right there is a gap leading into the next field. Go through the gap and immediately turn right to follow the wall to another dilapidated building this one being called Broad Law.

Go through the gateway in front of Broad Law and then bear left to head downhill towards the gate at the corner of the small clump of trees. See photo below. After going through the gate turn to the right and head towards the buildings of Eastgate House farm. As you get closer a gate becomes visible in the wall in front of the buildings. Head for the gate and pass through it and then go straight ahead towards the buildings, passing through a small wooden gate to enter the

Head to the left of the clump of trees below Broad Law.

farmyard. Go straight ahead passing between the buildings, ignore the access drive that turns to the left and keep straight on with the wall on the right. Go through the gate in front and once in the next field follow the wall on the left to be confronted by two gates in front of you. Go through the left hand gate and then look downhill and slightly to the left where you will see Eastgate Village Hall on the slopes below you. Head towards the building and you'll see what looks like a gate leading into the car park. It does actually lead onto a walled lane that passes in front of the Village Hall which was originally built as a girls' school in 1858 by the Hildyard family of Horsley Hall. Follow the lane past the Hall and the church on the left hand side to arrive in Eastgate. **GR 953 389.**

At this point you have the choice of route to either follow the shorter or the longer version of this walk. The shorter version turns left to return to Stanhope along the banks of the Wear whereas the longer version follows a loop up the valley of the Rookhope Burn before returning to Eastgate and then following the same route back to Stanhope as the shorter version.
To follow the shorter version turn left and walk down to meet the main A689 and then follow the directions as from point 7.
To follow the longer version follow the directions as from point 4 below.

4. Go straight across the road and up the path as indicated by the footpath sign. After a matter of literally a few feet turn right by the telegraph pole onto a path.

There is a footpath marker set high up on the pole and a couple of other markers along here to provide reassurance that you are on the right route. Follow the path as it leads you through the buildings to arrive at a footbridge over the Rookhope Burn. Cross the bridge and turn right to follow the path upstream. On the right is the first of a series of small waterfalls that you will pass as you head up the burn. Unfortunately the appearance of this one is rather spoilt by the large pipe crossing the burn just above it.

The waterfall underneath the footbridge as you cross the Rookhope Burn.

The path alongside the burn is a lovely walk and well worth the addition of the upper loop to your walk, however ,after a short distance you do have to leave the bank and walk through the caravan park that appears on your left. The way along the bank is blocked by rocks and sheer sides and so you have no choice but to go between the caravans. Walk right to the end of the park and pick up a clear path just after the last caravan.

The path is easy to follow as it follows the bank of the burn through fields and woods. At a couple of points in the woods erosion has made the path a little bit tricky but with care these shouldn't present much of an obstacle but at one point be aware that after crossing a side-stream a tree has fallen across the path and walkers have climbed up to go around it. At this point it is easy to lose the path but if you look carefully you will see it below you next to the burn.

Keep following the path along the bank until, while in an open area, you come

The banks of the Rookhope Burn.

to a point where a deep gully comes down to join the Rookhope and you have to cross it's stream at the gully mouth. If you look up you'll see a ruined wall running along the edge of the gully above you. Head up to the wall to find a path running in-between the wall and the gully. See photo over page. If you miss the wall and gully and continue following the bank you will shortly find your path blocked by a stone wall that has no way to cross it, in which case retrace your steps back to the gully and locate the wall.

Follow the path along the top of the gully, after a short distance the wall will end but keep following the edge of the gully to arrive at a gate leading onto the roadside. At the time of test walking this route this gate was very securely padlocked and so had to be climbed over. **GR 945 405.**

5. Turn left onto the road and follow it as it heads downhill back towards Eastgate. It is a quiet country road and gives some grand views over the lower reaches of the Rookhope Valley and Weardale. As you walk along the road you'll pass the entrance to South Hanging Wells Farm. Up on the hillside beyond the farm lies the remains of the prehistoric settlement of Hanging Wells, unfortunately it lies on private land so there is no opportunity to visit it. Follow the road downhill and on the outskirts of Eastgate pass the same caravan site that you walked through a couple of miles earlier. The road joins onto the main A689. **GR 952 387.**

The ruined wall running along the top of the gully, head up towards it to pick up the path.

6. At this junction turn left to pass in front of the Cross Keys pub and cross the road bridge over the Rookhope Burn. Just after the bridge is a second road junction, signposted to Eastgate Village Hall, this is the point where you rejoin the shorter route for the walk back to Stanhope. Before you cross the road have a look at the Roman altar next to the bus stop. See the next page for more details.

7. Cross the road to follow the footpath on the other side. After 1/4 mile there is a turning on the right, head down here and after crossing the bridge over the rail line come to the entrance to a caravan site with a Weardale Way signpost next to it. **GR 957 385.**

8. Walk down the tarmac access road for the caravan site and continue following it even when it turns right to go through the wall and into the site itself. The OS map shows the Way continuing to the end of the parameter wall and then between the rail line and the caravan site but this path is no longer possible due to an extension of the site and walking through it is the only viable option. Follow the access road for a short distance through the site to come to a metal gate at the end of the caravans. Go through the gate to find yourself next to the River Wear. The path from here back to Stanhope is relatively straight forward. The majority of the route lies between the rail line and the river and the land area is not large enough to make a mistake. At one point the path is directed round a house and then through a field at the end of which it arrives at a crossing point over the rail line itself. Safely across the railway the route follows a track past a large disused quarry to exit onto the roadside where the B6278 crosses the Wear. Staying on the left side of the river follow the road straight ahead to come to the A689 on the outskirts of Stanhope. Turn right and follow the road through Stanhope back to the Market Place.

The Roman Altar at Eastgate.

Set against the wall just in front of the bus shelter is a reproduction of a Roman altar found near to a millrace on the Rookhope Burn close to Eastgate. The original altar dates back to between AD 238 and 244 and is dedicated to Silvanus, the God of the woods.

The Roman footprint in Weardale was never very large although there was a presence close by at the nearby forts of Lanchester and Binchester which sat on the important military road of Dere Street. It appears that the dale was treated by the Romans as more of a hunting park rather than a place for permanent settlement and this is shown by the inscription carved on this altar and also on a similar one found in Bollihope.

Translated the inscription reads "To the God Silvanus, Aurelius Quirinus, Prefect, made this". Marcus Aurelius Quirinus was the prefect of a cohort of troops based at the Lanchester fort during the reign of Emperor Gordian III. He dedicated the altar to Silvanus as thanks for the successful hunting of an exceptionally large wild boar that had evaded other hunters.

The original altar is now in the Fulling Mill Museum in Durham.

THE BATTLE OF STANHOPE PARK.

Weardale may seem like a peaceful and tranquil place now but this was not always the case and surprisingly enough Stanhope features in the Wars of Scottish Independence.

By 1323 the long wars with Scotland were at a temporary end after the signing of the truce of Bishopthorpe. However in 1327 Edward II was forced to abdicate bringing to the throne of England his fourteen year old son Edward III but the real power lay with his mother Queen Isabella and her lover Roger Mortimer.

An attempt by Isabella and Mortimer to renew the existing truce led to an unintentional slight in the wording of the document. This suggested that the Scottish throne was subservient to the English which naturally upset the Scottish king, Robert Bruce, who was already distrustful of the intentions of the new regime anyway. However there were also deeper issues at stake with the ailing Bruce wanting to conclude his struggle for Scottish independence before he died. On the same day that Edward was crowned king of England, Bruce launched a surprise attack on Norham Castle in Northumberland thus ending the truce of Bishopthorpe.

On 15 June 1327 under the orders of Bruce a large cross-border raid was led by the Earl of Moray and Sir James Douglas. Weardale was particularly badly hit by the ravages and destruction caused by the Scots and while they were still making their way through the dale a large English army under the nominal command of the new boy-king Edward III left York to intercept them.

Typical Pennine weather of continuous rain made the pursuit of the Scots difficult partially due to the English troops being more heavily equipped than the lighter and more agile Scottish force. However on 1 August the English finally caught up with the invaders who were positioned on the southern bank of the River Wear and they in turn positioned themselves on the northern bank.

The Scots were in a good tactical position and resisted all attempts to draw them into battle but after a while they moved their force to take up an even stronger position at Stanhope Park, the hunting grounds of the Bishop of Durham. It was from here that on the night of 4 August the Lord Douglas led around two hundred men across the river in a surprise attack on the sleeping English army.

Taken completely off-guard the English were thrown completely into disarray. Accounts from the time state that upto three hundred English troops were killed, many while they still slept. The young Edward III only just managed to evade capture, being defended by his chaplain who was killed in the struggle.

After the assault the Scots withdrew back to their own positions where they stayed the following day. The next night the English had an anxious wait as they expected a further assault but despite frequent false alarms none came. The following night, 6 August, the Scots managed to outflank the English and escaped to the north. By the time that the English army had realised that the Scots had slipped away they were well on the way back to the border and pursuit was pointless.

So ended the Battle of Stanhope Park and from the English point of view an expensive fiasco. The whole Weardale campaign to pursue and defeat the Scots had cost £70,000 a staggering sum for the day and had ended up as a humiliating defeat for the English forces.

WALK 6: A WALK ROUND THE PARK

The Park Plantation and the farmland that it surrounds sits like an island in a sea of moor. This route takes a walk round the outside of the plantation, across the Stanhope Burn and up and along the edge of the moors above Crawley and Stanhope before descending back into the town.

DISTANCE: 6.9 mile (11.1 km)
ASCENT: 1,004 feet (306 metres)
TERRAIN: After a short road walk the majority of this walk is on moorland path but at times, as with all moorland paths, this can at various points develop into a quad track or just disappear all together. This route does include a crossing of the Stanhope Burn which in wet and bad weather may be hazardous.
TIME: 4.5 to 5.5 hours.
START: Stanhope Market Place. GR NY 996 391.
MAP: OL307 Consett & Derwent Reservoir.
DOGS: Allowed on the rights of way and I can't really see that there would be any problem over those stretches of access land used. At the most they account for two hundred metres to link rights of way. There are a number of awkward stiles to cross where the dog may have to be lifted over and there are sheep throughout the route plus a field of horses when you are coming off the moor near the B6278. You also pass through the middle of the animal sanctuary at Hope House.
ACCESS: Virtually all on public rights of way. There are one or two places where the route deviates from the right of way onto access land for short lengths just to make the walking easier.

Grid References

Stanhope Market Place	996 391
Road junction	983 394
Road/track junction	972 398
Gate	969 404
Track junction	975 423
Sheep pens	986 414
Track junction	991 415
Roadside	993 405
Gate	003 394
Stanhope Market Place	996 391

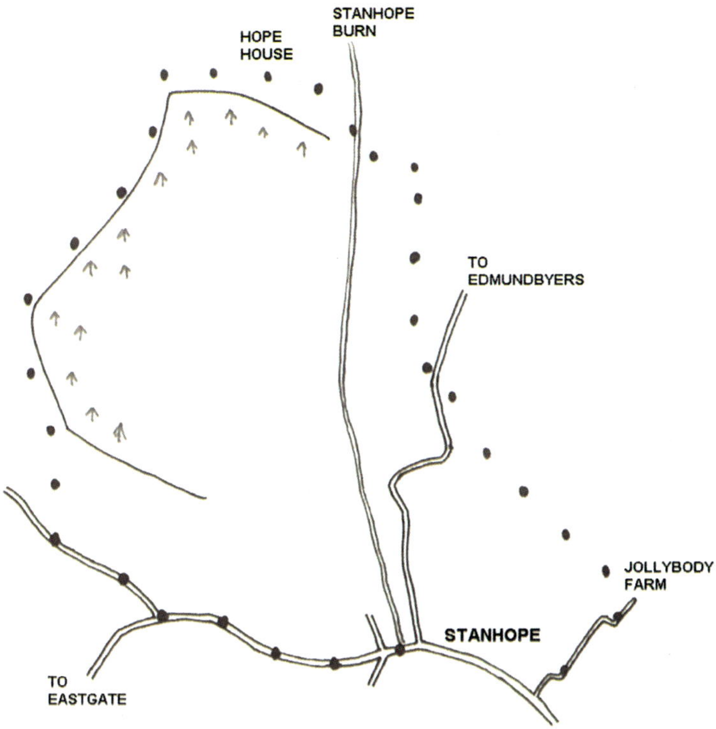

FGS Grading
Grading is F6 [D1, N1, T1, R1, H2]

Distance	**1**	6 – 12 miles
Navigation	**1**	Basic navigation skills needed
Terrain	**1**	50 – 75% on graded track or path 25 – 50% off track
Remoteness	**1**	Countryside in fairly close proximity to habitation – at least 80% of the route within 2 miles
Height	**2**	Over 125 ft per mile

THE WALK.

1. The first part of this walk, leaving Stanhope, is the same as the Eastgate Circular walk. From the Market Place leave Stanhope following the A689 to Alston. Walk on the right side of the road as there is footpath all the way. Go past the road junction where the B6278 goes off to the left and a smaller unclassified road goes off to the right. Continue following the A689 and 1/2 mile after leaving Stanhope and just past the sign for the Greenfoot Holiday Park there is a second unclassified road going off to the right, there is a blue cycle route sign for Rookhope pointing up it, see photo above. **GR 983 394.**

2. Turn right to head up this road and pass the entrances to the holiday park. The road steadily climbs but as it does it gives good views out over Weardale. After just over 1/4 mile, pass Greenhead Farm and shortly after that come to the first footpath sign on the right side of the road. Ignore this and after another 1/4 mile come to a second footpath sign on the right side of the road that points down a rough track. See top photo on opposite page. **GR 972 398.**

3. Turn right down the track to cross the thin stream and go through the gate onto the open moor. The track continues across the moor heading towards Park Plantation, the conifer woods in the distance. The track is easy enough to follow over the moor even when it leaves the guiding wall on the right. If in any doubt just head for the tree line. The track cuts across the moor to come to the perimeter wall that circles the plantation and arrives at the same gate that is used to enter the woods after coming down from the ridge line on the Crow Coal Hill walk. If you look to the left you can see the trig point on Crow Coal summit. **Gate GR 969 404.**

The track leaving the road and heading towards Park Plantation.

4. Ignore the gate and start to follow the outside of the wall straight ahead. Navigation on this next stretch is very easy as you are just walking round the outside of the plantation. The route round the outside is a footpath and for most of the way there is a recognisable path although for some parts it gets "lost" amongst

Following the outside of Park Plantation.

the vegetation and in others it becomes more of a track.

As you follow the wall the route crosses five water courses, most are small and you'd probably not even notice them. However the fifth and last one, the Reahope Burn, is more substantial and will be noticed as you drop down to its gully to cross. As you've been approaching the Reahope Burn you'll probably have seen the slim shape of an unnamed currick on the skyline of Gibb Hill. If you fancy a diversion feel free to make the short climb to visit it. Its easy enough to relocate back to the route of the walk, just head downhill towards the trees.

Shortly after crossing the Reahope you'll come to a large fenced area. It isn't until you get relatively close that you start to get an inkling what is on the other side of the fence, a fairly deep hole in the ground that is a disused quarry. As you get up to the fence you'll find a section of the wire has been snipped to make a gap for the farmer's quad. There is a corresponding gap on the other side of the enclosure presumably to save the farmer having to drive all the way round this large area. There is plenty of room to safely make your way round the deep hole and through the gap on the other side although in poor visibility I'd maybe be a bit more cautious.

The disused quarry on the outside of the plantation. Originally the footpath ran alongside the wall but that has long since disappeared into the hole.

Continue following the wall and eventually the path starts to develop into a more substantial track. Shortly after this the edge of the wood makes a sharp right hand corner and the track continues straight on. The OS map shows the footpath turning the corner and continuing to follow the outside of the wall however on the ground there is no visible path and it is quite rough going. The better option is to stay on the track for the next couple of hundred yards until you come to a T-junction with another track. **GR 975 423.**

5. Turn right onto this new track and follow it downhill. From the track you do get quite extensive views of the valley of the Stanhope Burn. You'll get closer to the burn itself a little bit later. Ignore the track on the right that shoots off into the woods and continue on the main track until it comes to a junction where a red "Animal Ambulance" is normally parked, it actually looks as if it has never moved for a considerable time.

Approaching the junction above Hope House with the animal ambulance.

Here the track bears right to go through a gate into the trees and also goes left to head across the moor. Bear left and at the end of the wall turn right to descend to Hope House. Pass through the gated entrance and almost immediately start looking on the right for a small wooden stile crossing the wire fence. Be careful on the stile as there is no support to hold onto and the stile itself is a bit wobbly. Once across the stile head down hill to the right hand corner of the field to find another more substantial stile to cross. Cross and continue heading downhill keeping the wall on the right. When the wall bends away to the right continue going straight down to find another stile that gives access to the banks of the Stanhope Burn. Cross the burn, you may have to move up or downstream to find a suitable spot and then when across, follow the burn downstream to arrive at a collection of sheep pens next to a bridge. **GR 986 414.**

In the 19th century the valley of the Stanhope Burn was a hive of industry including a high concentration of lead mines and their associated activities. The ruined buildings seen on the other side of the sheep pens are the remains of a more modern site that was used to extract the mineral fluorspar from the old lead mines and was active up to the 1970's. However prior to 1875 it was a lead smelting mill that used to be sited next to the burn, smelting being that part of the process that extracted the lead from the rock ore. The Stanhopeburn Smelting Mill was a sizeable operation not only processing the ore from the mines in this valley but also from the whole area including the mines from over the hill in Rookhope.

With so much industrial activity taking place on the one spot it is difficult to identify the remains of individual buildings and processes but as you start to

The remains of the old flue system from Stanhopeburn lead smelting mill making its way up the side of the hillside.

climb the Velvet Path, on the left hand side of the track you can still identify stone forms and shapes from the outbuildings of the old smelting mill including the remains of the long flue that was used to take the poisonous fumes away from the smelter and up the hillside to be released high above the moor.

6. The sheep pens will no doubt look familiar and so they should as this spot is passed on two of the other walks in this book and in both these cases you pass through the red hurdles onto the road. This time go through them off the road and turn left to head steeply uphill keeping on the left of the wall. One short but steep climb later and you join the Velvet Path as it comes through a gate in the wall. Staying on the left side of this wall follow the path as it climbs uphill. A 1/4 mile later the wall does a 90 degree turn to the right to head away from the track and at this point there is a discernable track starting to follow it.
GR 991 415.

The Velvet Path heading uphill.

7. Turn right to leave the Velvet Path and descend down to the Heathery Burn. The waters are a distinct red oxide colour possibly from iron deposits further upstream and they are very unheathery looking. Cross the stream and climb the steep hill following the wall on the right. The climb soon levels out and the path is not bad walking and soon joins a quad track that is heading in the same direction. While you are walking take the opportunity to look over the wall on the left to see the majority of the route that you have just walked laid out in front of you. Keep following the track alongside the wall and 1/2 mile later as you are approaching the buildings at Crawley Engine the track takes a sharp left hand turn but continue straight on to the wall in front to find a small wooden gate in the wall corner. Go through the gate which is the first in a series of three and pass the house to head to the roadside. At the roadside there is another small wooden gate at 90 degrees to the metal gate in front of you. Go through the gate to arrive at the roadside. **GR 993 405.**

8. Cross the road to the footpath sign opposite, see photo below, but before continuing the walk take the time to look over the wall on the left.

What you see here is all that is left of the Crawleyside Incline, part of a rail system that used to carry limestone from the quarries surrounding Stanhope to the ironworks at Consett and the ports on the Tyne. Here the incline is emerging from a tunnel built under the road and then going through the cutting to Crawley Engine. The incline itself was too steep for locomotive engines and so a stationary steam engine was used to pull the laden wagons by rope, up from the quarries below. Once at the engine the wagons would then be pulled by a similar arrangement up to the Weatherhill Engine further up the line before being connected to a locomotive.

Crossing the road to the footpath on the other side.

Go through the gate indicated by the footpath sign and follow the path as it heads alongside the fence which quickly becomes a wall. You soon come to a more defined path heading from left to right. Bear right to join this and continue in the same basic direction as you were heading.

The path now follows the top of Crawley Edge and its crags, below lies Stanhope and a vast area of old quarry workings. Now grassed over, the sheer size of the workings shows the importance quarrying had on the economy and development of Stanhope. Continue walking along the top of the Edge ignoring the three paths that join on from the right and head downhill. You may not notice the first path as it comes in at an angle from behind you but the second and third are easily recognised. After 1/2 mile the path starts a gentle descent and shortly passes to the right of a walled enclosure with a set of ruins behind the wall, see photo below. As you pass the path develops into a stony track but continue following and the track comes to a gate in a wall on the right of the buildings of Hill Crest. **GR 003 394.**

Descending down past the enclosure and ruins.

9. Go through the gate and turn right onto the tarmac road. Follow the road down into Stanhope and when you get to the main road turn right again to arrive back at the Market Place.

WALK 7: FROSTERLEY CIRCUIT

A shorter walk that takes a circular route along the edge of the moors and fields on the north side of the river to Frosterley and then returns on the south side skirting the hillside of Catterick before descending through the fields for a short riverside walk back to Stanhope.

DISTANCE: 7.6 mile (12.2 km)
ASCENT: 1,555 feet (474 metres)
TERRAIN: A walk that flits between the edges of the moors and the fields below. Most of the walk is over rough pasture whether it is on the edge of the moor or in the fields although a rough track is followed over the edge of the moors leading from Hill End.
TIME: 3 to 4 hours.
START: Stanhope Market Place. GR NY 996 391.
MAP: OL31 North Pennines Teesdale and Weardale.
DOGS: As the route is entirely over public rights of way then dogs are allowed under close control. Be aware that there are some narrow stiles built into walls on this route that may require lifting the dog over and that there are a couple of sections along public roads. Livestock will be encountered throughout the route and you do pass through the middle of a caravan site.
ACCESS: This route is all on public rights of way.
REFRESHMENTS ON ROUTE: The Black Bull in Frosterley.

Grid References

Stanhope Market Place	996 391
Road/footpath junction	001 393
Stile in wall	009 389
Track crossroads	010 389
Road junction	021 372
Road/footpath junction	022 365
Telephone box	015 361
Gate in wall	002 364
Footpath/road junction	001 382
Stanhope Market Place	996 391

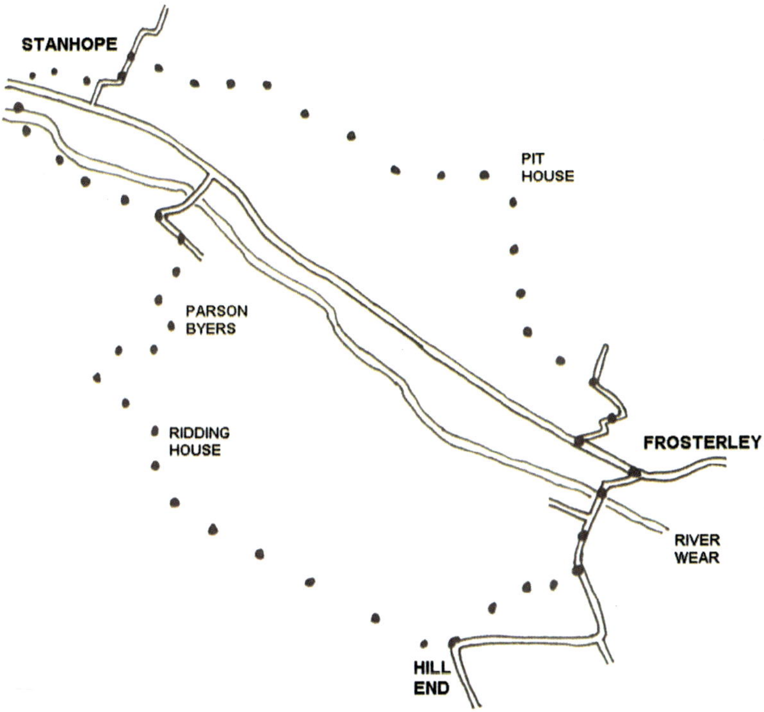

FGS Grading

Grading is F8 [D1, N2, T2, R1, H2]

Distance	1	6 – 12 miles
Navigation	**2**	Competent navigation skills needed
Terrain	**2**	25 -50% on graded track or path 50 – 75% off / single track
Remoteness	**1**	Countryside in fairly close proximity to habitation – at least 80% of the route within 2 miles
Height	**2**	Over 125 ft per mile

THE WALK.

1. The first part of this walk follows the same route out of Stanhope as the Fatherley Hill walk. So from the market place head up the lane between the church and the Bonny Moorhen pub. See the photo on page 27. At the top of the lane turn right and follow the road past two turnings on the right and where the third road comes in on the right bear left to follow it steeply uphill until you come to a footpath sign on the right side of the road and a stile in the wall. See photo on page 47. **GR 001 393.**

2. Cross the stile to enter the field and then follow the fence and in front of you will appear two gates. Head to the left hand gate and you'll find the first of a series of newly constructed wooden kissing gates. Pass through and continue following the wall to pass through a second and then a third gate. After passing through the third gate the wall on the right has disappeared and you are faced with an open field. Instead of taking the obvious route straight ahead to the gate opposite, bear to the left towards the corner of the field to find another one of the new kissing gates. Pass through and straight in front see a stile over a wire fence that runs along the top of the valley of the Shittlehope Burn. Cross the stile and descend the steep path down to the footbridge that spans the burn.

Cross the bridge and climb the other side and where the path branches take the left hand fork to leave the valley. Cross the stile over the wire fence and head towards the wall on the right where there is a gap and a waymarker post.

There is a nice boggy bit of ground on the other side of the gap but once past that head in the direction indicated by the waymarker going to the left of the trees and between the two ruins, see photo on page 48, where the path climbs a small rise and arrives at a stile in the wall on the left of an old barn.
GR 009 389.

3. The stile gives access to the open moor and once across turn left to follow the path as it heads uphill. As the path reaches the lip of the climb it forms a cross-roads with another faint path that is running along the edge of the escarpment. Go straight on and in a short distance you will meet a vehicle track, turn right to follow this track. As you walk along the track keep your eyes open for small earthworks running alongside the track and in some cases the track cuts through them. Standing only about a foot or so high these are the remains of field boundaries that date back to the prehistoric, possibly the Bronze Age. Sounds strange but four thousand years ago when the climate was milder this moorland was capable of providing good farmland that sustained a substantial and wealthy population. Keep following the track until you come to a crossroads formed by another track coming up from the farm below you and then heading up to the top of the moor. **GR 010 389.**

4. At the crossroads continue straight on and after a short distance a faint track leads off on the left while the main track bends away to the right. Follow this faint track uphill, although faint it is relatively easy to follow. Eventually it meets a more pronounced track coming in from the left and here you turn right to follow it as it runs across the slope of the hill heading towards the wall in the distance where you'll find a gate.

After going through the gate bear left to the 10 o'clock position to find a stile over the fence. In this next field there are two prominent stream gullies, head uphill to follow the first gully to a gate in the fence above you. Once through the gate turn right to follow the fence line past the front of the ruins of Pit House to come to a stile in the wall. Cross the stile and bear right to head downhill keeping a short distance from the wall on the right until you can see a stile in the wall ahead.

The ruins of Pit House.

Cross the stile and continue heading downhill, crossing the tarmac drive to the left of Frosterley Cottage and make directly for the centre of the clump of trees in front of you, see photo overleaf. In the trees you'll pick up an old trackway that bears to the left to come to a stile in the wall bordering the trees. Head straight across the next field making for the blue gate through which you pass to

Heading downhill to the left of Frosterley Cottage.

arrive on a tarmac road. Turn right and follow this road downhill until you come to the main A689 road on the outskirts of Frosterley. **GR 021 372.**

5. Turn left at the road and head down into Frosterley until you come to the junction with the White Kirkley and Hill End road. Turn right to follow this road and pass Frosterley Station and the Black Bull Inn. Mind you, its not compulsory to pass the Black Bull, they do great meals and it makes a good lunch stop. I've got to admit I do have a weakness for their real ginger beer. Anyway, whether you stop first or not, continue following the road over the bridge crossing the Wear and up through Bridge End. Keep heading uphill on the road till just past the school and here there is a house on the right side of the road with a footpath sign pointing up its drive. **GR 022 365.**

6. Cross the road to go through the gate and walk up the gravel drive to the second gate and then into the field, see photo below. Follow the fence line on the left to go through a gateway and then keeping the ditch and old fence line still on the left, walk round the edge of the next couple of fields as they make a dog leg and then come to a stile in the corner of the field. Cross the stile and ignoring the footpath sign on the right, continue straight uphill keeping the wall on the right. At the top of the hill are the houses of Hill End and at the end of the field the path comes to a black metal kissing gate which leads on to a short lane between them to arrive at the roadside next to a telephone box.
GR 015 361.

Walking up the very well laid out gravel drive.

7. Turn right onto the road and follow it past the houses. As you leave Hill End ignore the first footpath sign and cross the cattle grid. You then come to a second footpath sign that is also a Weardale Way signpost, turn onto the track indicated by the sign and follow it as it heads uphill for a short distance and starts to run alongside a wall on the right. This track is now followed for the next mile as it follows the wall. Eventually the track comes to a small gate in a wall corner complete with Weardale Way marker post. **GR 002 364.**

8. Continue following the Weardale Way and go through the gate to follow the left hand wall down through the field. At the bottom of the field go through the stile next to the gate with the Weardale Way marker pointing straight on. This will bring you out on a crossroads and here you go straight on through the gate in front despite the fact that it has no marker on. One word of caution, when the walk was tested this gate was tied tightly shut and had to be climbed. Once through the gate head towards the farm of Ridding House that you could see over the rise of the hill and pick up a track which goes to an open gateway to the left of the building.

Go through the gateway and immediately turn left to follow a trackway to the end of the field. Go through the gate and continue following the track. This track soon disappears in the field being replaced by a number of paths and sheep trods. As you walk, slowly bear to the right making your way to the fence that runs along the edge of the field above the quarry.

Follow the fence line to the point where you descend to cross a dry stream bed and once across climb the steep bank and as you do so follow the wall in front as it bears to the left to come to a gap between the wall and a fenced enclosure that surrounds what appears to be an old shaft. Go through the gap to arrive at a gate in the right hand wall, pass through the gate and cut through the field heading towards the fence opposite, which again runs along the top of the quarry. Follow the fence round the quarry's edge and a track materialises which is followed through some old workings. At one point the track gets a bit difficult to identify but follow a line of trees to arrive at a gate. Go through the gate and turn left onto the track on the other side and this will slowly descend to a crossroads.

Following the track through the old quarry workings.

Go straight over the crossroads to come to the buildings of Parson Byers where the track takes a sharp turn to the right. At this point there is a very prominent footpath marker pointing over the fields but ignore this and continue on the track as it passes to the left of the buildings. Just past the last building the wall on the left has a gate and stile proudly carrying the Weardale Way marker, go over the stile and follow the obvious path running diagonally across the field and heading towards the row of houses on the road below. Cross the stile opposite the houses to join the road. **GR 001 382.**

9. Turn left and follow the road. When you come to the entrance to the Heather View Holiday Park, the Weardale Way continues straight on through the park as shown by the signpost. So pass through the park's entrance and follow the tarmac road straight on as it makes its way through the caravans passing the reception hut on the right and then a little bit later a large grey metal building also on the right. Shortly after this building the road starts to bear to the left and at this point the Weardale Way and yourself continue straight ahead through a wooden gate following a track with fields on one side and woods on the other, see photo below.

The wooded lane leaving the caravan park.

Follow the track as it starts to descend to the fields below and pass through the gate to enter a field. Continue to follow the wall on the left until you come to a wall corner where the wall turns to the left. At this point you have a route choice, the Weardale Way turns left to follow the wall or alternatively you can go straight ahead to join a riverside path that heads upstream. My personal choice would be the riverside path but it is a bit academic anyway as both paths join together shortly before a footbridge over the Wear. Cross the bridge and turn right to follow the tarmac path alongside the river and when it meets the bottom of The Butts follow the road back upto the Market Place and the end of the walk.

WALK 8: ROOKHOPE CIRCULAR

A longer walk using the little-used estate track to cross the moors between Stanhope and the Rookhope Valley. From the village of Rookhope the Weardale Way is followed back to Stanhope with a short road walk leading to a delightful stretch following the Rookhope Burn downstream through fields and woods to Eastgate. A riverside path along the banks of the Wear then returns the walker to Stanhope.

DISTANCE: 12.6 mile (20.2 km)
ASCENT: 1,362 feet (415 metres)
TERRAIN: A mix ranging from moorland path and track in the first half of the walk to field and woodland paths in the later stages, including a short stretch of road walking when leaving Rookhope.
TIME: 5.5 to 6.5 hours.
START: Stanhope Market Place. GR NY 996 391.
MAP: OL307 Consett & Derwent Reservoir.
DOGS: Not allowed on the access land due to conservation issues.
ACCESS: Most of this route is on public rights of way although there is a sizeable stretch following the track from Stanhope Common over the ridgeline into the Rookhope Valley that is on public access land.
REFRESHMENTS ON ROUTE: Rookhope Inn in the village of Rookhope.

Grid References

Stanhope Market Place	996 391
Gate	996 399
Track/railway junction	994 407
Road/track junction	995 414
Sheep pens	986 414
Gate	982 419
Rookhope	939 429
Footbridge	944 416
Road junction	953 387
Caravan site entrance	957 385
Stanhope Market Place	996 391

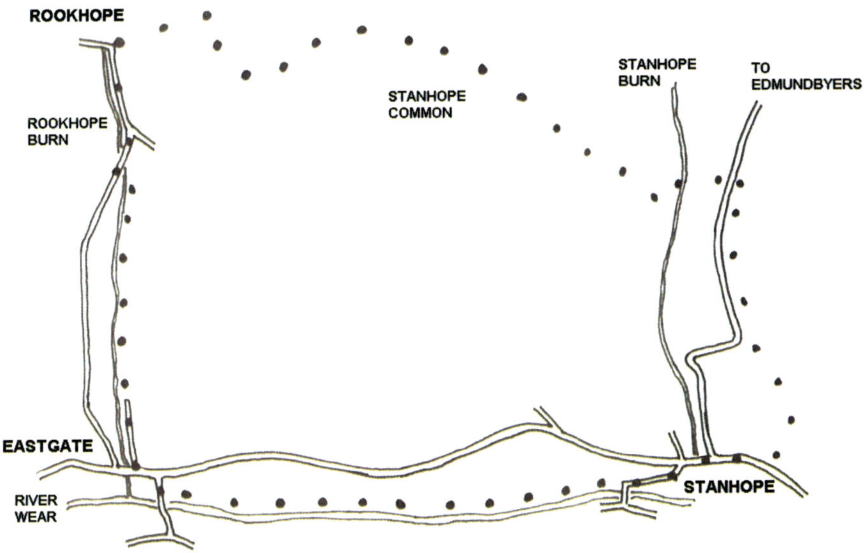

FGS Grading
Grading is F6 [D2, N1, T1, R1, H1]

Distance	**2**	12 – 18 miles
Navigation	**1**	Basic navigation skills needed
Terrain	**1**	50 – 75% on graded track or path 25 – 50% off track
Remoteness	**1**	Countryside in fairly close proximity to habitation – at least 80% of the route within 2 miles
Height	**1**	Over 100 ft per mile

THE WALK.

1. The first part of this route follows the same paths up Crawleyside as the Collier Law walk so from the Market Place head up the lane between the church and The Bonny Moorhen pub, see photo on page 27. At the top of the lane turn left to walk down the road and just after Stanhope Methodist Church take the footpath on the right leading up between the buildings towards the moors. Go through the small gate and follow the path straight on over a crossroads before crossing two bridges spanning the old quarry workings. Go through another small gate and then follow the fence as it bears left to run above the quarries. This is a nice green path running alongside the fence but shortly you'll spy a cottage on the slopes above and another path that leaves the fence and heads up towards a gate in the wall leading to the cottage. Climb up to the gate, see photo on page 28. **GR 996 399.**

2. Go through the gate and also the second gate next to it to get onto the moor. Turn left and follow the path as it heads up the side of the hill. As you reach the lip of the hill a path comes in from the right, it is hard to decide whether this path is joining you or you are joining it, but keep going in the same direction. As you walk along you'll find two paths heading off to the left, the second one being close to some ruins and has a prominent waymarker that could confuse. However stay on the current path as it curves round and heads towards the walls that surround the buildings of the old Crawley Engine site. Follow the wall around the buildings to come onto a track where you bear left and after a hundred yards or so this bring you to the bottom of a disused railway line, just before you come to the main B6278 road. **GR 994 407.**

3. Turn right and follow the rail track uphill passing the disused Crawley Reservoir as you do. After 1/2 mile a walled enclosure appears on the left side of the track bed and as the enclosure ends a vehicle track cuts across the old rail line and heads up Bashaw Rigg. This is the track used on the Collier Law walk. Go past this track and after a short distance another track bears to the left to meet the B6278 road with a footpath sign and the start of a track on the other side of the road. **GR 995 414.**

4. Cross the road and start to descend on the track down to the valley of the Stanhope Burn. Along the way pass a metal seat erected in memory of WO Colin Wall, one of our servicemen killed in Basra during the Iraq conflict. This track is known locally as the Velvet Path due to its soft grassy surface however in places this has long gone and the surface is quiet stony and wet. A small bridge brings you onto the right side of the Heathery Burn and as you descend you pass a series of small quarries on the right. The exact location is not known but in this area the famous Heathery Burn Hoard was found during the 1800's hidden in a cave that was excavated during quarrying, see page 90. Follow the track down and where it turns to the left to pass through the wall leave the track and staying on the right side of the wall to take the steep descent down to the sheep pens next to the bridge over the Stanhope Burn. Next to the pens a couple of red metal hurdles act as a gate through the fence onto the road. **GR 986 414.**

The Stanhope Burn from the bridge next to the sheep pens.

5. Turn right onto the road to cross the bridge and start heading uphill. As you climb come to a junction on the right with a collection of wheelie bins, bear right to go under the trees and come out onto a track with fields to the left and woods to the right. This section of the walk covers part of the same route as the Crow Coal Hill walk so may be familiar if you have already done that one. Continue up the track and as the buildings of High House come into view turn right to follow the track through the woods to the gate leading onto the open moor. **GR 982 419.**

6. Go through the gate and ignoring the track going straight-on, bear to the left to follow the main track as it heads uphill across the open moor. As you walk away from the woods there are two tracks that leave the main track and head back to the woods, stay on the obvious main track. Follow this track to the shooting lodge, through it's plantation and up to the ridgeline with its burial mounds. Instead of turning off to follow the ridge as you did on the Crow Coal Hill walk, stay on the track to descend the other side of the ridge into the Rookhope Valley. The track doesn't descend directly into the valley, instead it curves to contour round the slopes of Long Law until it comes to a junction with an old trackway.

This trackway was once part the main artery for the mines of Rookhope taking their produce to the shipping centres of Tyneside. Now it is part of the popular Coast to Coast Cycle Way and if you're lucky you'll spy one or two mountain bikers breathing hard as they try to pedal up this steep incline.

Turn left to follow the trackway down into Rookhope to arrive at the main street. **GR 939 429.**

A rather artistic waymarker for the cyclist's Coast to Coast route, found just as you enter Rookhope.

7. If you fancy a lunch break at the Rookhope Inn turn right to find it just round the corner. To continue on the route turn left to follow the road along the main street and out of Rookhope heading towards Eastgate and the Wear Valley. Follow the road as it makes its way alongside the Rookhope Burn. When you get to the houses of Stotfield Burn there is a road junction but stay on the main road until you come to a bridge spanning the Rookhope Burn which is where you leave the road to follow the Weardale Way down to Eastgate. At this point the OS map shows the Way leaving the road before the bridge and heading down the left bank of the burn however this no longer applies as the left bank has been badly hit by erosion. Instead cross the road bridge and shortly after come to a Weardale Way signpost pointing to a footbridge across the burn, see photo below. **GR 944 416.**

The footbridge crossing the Rookhope Burn.

8. Cross the footbridge to arrive on the left side of the Rookhope Burn and start to follow the burn downstream however at this point a wire fence does prevent you from actually walking next to the stream. You soon come to a very soggy bit where a stream flows through the field on its way to the burn and gives the majority of this field the texture of a paddy field. It may be possible to go high and avoid the worst of the wet but I just delicately tip-toed through the mire. Continue walking downstream and you'll come to a post with a Weardale Way marker on it. At first sight this is confusing as it seems to point in the direction of heading uphill, however, ignore this and stay close to the burn and enter the woods bordering the stream. As you walk through the woods you'll pass a series of ruined walls and buildings that formed part of the quarry workings lying further uphill. Long abandoned they have over the years been slowly reclaimed by the woods.

Eventually the woods give way to an open space where a side valley descends to join the Rookhope and here the path moves away from the burn to cross a footbridge over the tributary. The path now re-enters a short stretch of woodland and when it comes out in to the open again, it begins to climb away from the burn until it comes to a point above a flat terrace which lies next to a large bend in the stream. Here the path starts to descend down to the terrace but instead of going all the way down the slope it curves round the right side of a stone wall to meet an old track and start to climb again heading for a fence corner and a Weardale Way marker. Follow the fence keeping it on the right and the path develops into a track and enters another stretch of woodland.

The path through the woods alongside the Rookhope Burn.

The track leaves the wood at Hole House where it joins a decent farm track for the next stretch to Holm House where it changes to tarmac and heads down into Eastgate. Go past the buildings of Eastgate to arrive at the main A689 road. **GR 953 387.**

9. From here the walk follows the Weardale Way back to Stanhope and is the same route as used in the Eastgate Circular walk. Turn left and cross the road to follow the footpath on the other side. After 1/4 mile there is a turning on the right, head down here and after crossing the bridge over the rail line come to the entrance to a caravan site with a Weardale Way signpost next to it. **GR 957 385.**

10. Walk down the tarmac access road for the caravan site and continue following it even when it turns right to go through the wall and into the site itself. The OS map shows the Way continuing to the end of the parameter wall and then between the rail line and the caravan site but this path is no longer possible due to an extension of the site and walking through it is the only viable option. Follow the access road for a short distance through the site to come to a metal gate at the end of the caravans. Go through the gate to find yourself next to the River Wear. The path from here back to Stanhope is relatively straight forward. The majority of the route lies between the rail line and the river and the land area is not large enough to make a mistake. At one point the path is directed round a house and then through a field at the end of which it arrives at a crossing point over the rail line itself. Safely across the railway the route follows a track past a large disused quarry to exit onto the roadside where the B6278 crosses the Wear. Staying on the left side of the river follow the road straight ahead to come to the A689 on the outskirts of Stanhope. Turn right and follow the road through Stanhope back to the Market Place.

One of the old quarries alongside the Velvet Path. It was while excavating one of these that the Heathery Burn Hoard was found in the 1800's.

THE HEATHERY BURN HOARD .

It may seem out of place situated where it is but close to the Velvet Path as it runs alongside the Heathery Burn, was discovered one of the most important Bronze Age finds in the country. During quarrying operations during the 1800's a large cave was discovered and between 1859 and 1872 a number of late Bronze Age objects were recovered from it. The Bronze Age period ran from 2,300 BC to 800 BC and even though these artefacts were late Bronze Age this would still make them around 3,000 to 4,000 years old.

The objects were recovered over a number of years but sadly many of the earlier finds have disappeared and are now untraceable. Those parts of the Hoard that have survived are now on display in the British Museum.

In terms of the historical perspective the contents of the Hoard are quite significant including evidence of the earliest use of wheeled vehicles from anywhere in the British Isles. Included in the Hoard were two gold ornaments, a large number of bronze rings, pins, spearheads, swords, axes, armlets and a bucket. Also found were a collection of flint flakes and barbed and tanged arrowheads showing that the inhabitants hadn't quite left the stone age behind although it is known from other finds around the country that the defining line between stone and bronze is not clear-cut and the use of flint tools extended long into the period of metal use.

Human skeletons were also uncovered along with pottery and animal bones. The discovery of human remains laid within a cave is not unique either nationally or even within County Durham. A cave on the Durham coast at Ryhope Dene contained the skeletons of six adults and one child although no artefacts were found, any there having long since been plundered. Another cave was excavated at Bishop Middleham in 1932 this time with the remains of eleven skeletons and in this case with a small number of late Bronze Age artefacts. A further find at Walker's Quarry close to Ferryhill yielded four skeletons but few artefacts. So there does appear to be a practice of laying the dead to rest in caves along with a deliberate placement of their belongings. Maybe the cave was considered to be a sacred place and was used to help the dead through the gateway to the next life.

Whether this was a place of burial with the bodies interred with grave goods or there was another reason why this collection was placed here we'll never know. However the wealth contained within the Heathery Burn Hoard does help to cement the theory that the area around Stanhope was a rich and vibrant society three to four thousand years ago.

APPENDIX

Ferguson Grading System (`FGS`)

1. Introduction
The FGS has been adopted as a means of assessing the nature and severity of the various walks in this book and the abilities and equipment needed to tackle each one safely. The FGS was developed by Stuart Ferguson, a long time fell and trail runner, climber, mountaineer, mountain-biker and general outdoor enthusiast. In the opinion of Trailguides the FGS is the most accurate and comprehensive grading system for comparing off-road walking, running and mountain-biking routes anywhere in the country.

2. The System
Tables 1 & 2, set out below, are used in order to give a grading to each route. Table 1 sets out three categories of country that a route could potentially cross, together with a range of factors that would need to be considered when tackling that route. The three categories are, Trail, Fell and Mountain, and after assessing which category best fits the route, a letter, either `T`, `F` or `M`, is allocated to that route. Where a route does not fit perfectly into one of the three categories the closest category is allocated.

Table 2 deals with five specific aspects of the route, distance, navigation, terrain, remoteness and height gain, and each one is allocated a letter, `D`, `N`, `T`, `R`, and `H`. Each letter is also given a severity score from the range 0-3 or 0-4, in respect of distance (`D`). The higher the number, the more severe the route. The five severity scores are then added together to give an overall score. The overall score is then put with the Table 1 category letter (i.e. `T`, `F` or `M`).

In order to show how the grading has been determined for each walk in this book, the five individual severity scores are set out, in square brackets, immediately after the actual grading. So, for example, Walk 8 Rookhope Circular has a grading of F6 [D2, N1, T1, R1, H1], indicating that it is a Fell Category walk with a total severity score of 6. This is made up of the five specific severity scores, for distance (`D`), navigation (`N`), terrain (`T`), remoteness (`R`) and height gain (`H`), of 2, 1, 1, 1 and 1 respectively. The highest total severity score which can be achieved is 16 and the lowest total severity score achievable is 0.

The table which accompanies the grading for each walk sets out the specific factors, extracted from Table 2, that need to be considered when tackling that particular walk.

TABLE 1

	TRAIL	FELL	MOUNTAIN
Description	Lowland and forest areas including urban, cultivated and forested locations.	Moorlands and upland areas which may include some upland cultivated and forestry areas plus possibly remote locations.	Upland and mountain areas including remote and isolated locations.
Height	Not usually above 1,000 feet but may go up to 2,500 feet	Usually above 1,000 feet, up to 2,500 feet and above.	Usually above 2,500 feet and up to 4,000 feet.
Way-marking	Usually	Limited	None
Terrain	Usually graded paths, tracks and trails but may include some off-trail	May include some graded paths, tracks and trails but mainly off-trail	Virtually all off-trail
Height gain	Limited height gain	May include considerable height gain	May include some severe height gain.
Effects of weather	Very limited effect	May be prone to sudden weather changes	Extreme weather a possibility
Navigational skills	None to basic	Basic to competent	Competent to expert
Equipment	Walking shoes/boots. Possibly waterproofs Food and drink dependant upon route.	3/4 season walking boots. Full waterproof cover. Possibly map and compass dependant upon route. Food and drink dependant upon route.	Mountain boots. Full waterproof cover. Map and compass. Food and drink
Escape Routes	Yes	Some	Some to nil

TABLE 2

Score	**0**	**1**	**2**	**3**	**4**
Distance	Up to 6 miles	6 – 12 miles	12 – 18 miles	18 miles +	24 miles +
Navigation	No navigation skills needed	Basic navigation skills needed	Competent navigation skills needed	Expert navigation skills needed	
Terrain	75% + on graded track or path	50 – 75% on graded track or path 25 – 50% off track	25 -50% on graded track or path 50 – 75% off track	Under 25% on graded track or path Over 75% off track	
Remoteness	Urban	Countryside in fairly close proximity to habitation – at least 80% of the route within 2 miles	Countryside not in close proximity to habitation – less than 20% of the route within 2 miles	Remote, isolated location	
Height gain	Less than 100 ft per mile	Over 100 ft per mile	Over 125 ft per mile	Over 250 ft per mile	

Notes to Table 2

Graded paths = Well established paths with a stable surface.

Escape routes = The opportunity to cut the route short and return to the start without completing the full course in the event of weather changes or unforeseen incidents.

The Author

Keven Shevels

Kev has been involved with outdoor sports for over forty years since his school days doing the Duke of Edinburgh award, spending his time either walking, running and latterly mountain biking through the countryside of the North East and beyond. He is not ashamed to admit that he is one of these boring people who can sit and spend hours reading a map the way that other people read a book.

His great delight is coming up with new routes that he can subsequently explore and investigate especially if he can couple this with his interest in history, in particular the prehistoric. This usually means much more than a walk as his routes tend to take a view not only on the landscape but also its relationship with events and occurrences that have happened in the past. In many ways this curiosity and knowledge of the Durham Dales can make him a perfect guide to this under-valued part of our region.

Now in his fifties, Kev has been unable to continue his running due to injury problems but instead has been co-author of one of the most innovative series of coaching books for fell and trail runners in recent years. He now brings his easy to read, informative style of writing to guide books for those who walk in the countryside of County Durham, his home county.

The author having a break out in the Durham countryside.

Walking North East

Walking North East is the brand name for the walking publications produced by Trailguides and reflects the pride that we, as North Easterners, have in our countryside, our history and our culture.

Based in Darlington, we are a small independent publisher specialising in guidebooks centred on the North Eastern counties of England. Our target is to produce guides that are as user-friendly, easy to use and provide as much information as possible and all in an easily readable format. In essence to increase the enjoyment of the user and to showcase the very best of the great North Eastern countryside. Our series of books explores the heritage of us all and lets you see your region with new eyes, these books are written to not just take you on a walk but to investigate, explore and understand the objects, places and history that has shaped not just the countryside but also the people of this corner of England.

If you've enjoyed following the routes in this guide and want news and details of other publications that are being developed under the Walking North East label then look at the company website at **www.trailguides.co.uk**

Comments and, yes, criticisms, are always welcomed especially if you discover a change to a route. Contact us by email through the website or by post at Trailguides Limited, 35 Carmel Road South, Darlington, Co Durham DL3 8DQ.

Other walking books from Walking North East.
At the time of publication the following books are also available but with new titles being regularly added to our publication list keep checking our website.

Northumberland.
The Cheviot Hills.
Kielder Castle.
Walks from Wooler.
The Hills of Upper Coquetdale.
Walks from Kirknewton.

County Durham.
Hamsterley Forest.
The Barningham Trail.
Ancient Stones.
The High Hills of Teesdale.
Walks from Stanhope.
Mid-Teesdale Walks.

North Yorkshire.
The Hills of Upper Swaledale.

Walking North East.
Visit our website and sign up to receive our free newsletter, Walking North East, dedicated to walking in North Eastern England. Full of news, views and articles relating to this the forgotten corner of England.

Acknowledgements.
Are due to Harry Manuel for accompanying me on these walks and for being a fundamental part of the route testing procedure while occasionally appearing as the "model" in some of the photographs. Thanks are also due to my wife Lyn for the patience and tolerance shown while I "disappear" to walk and write about these routes.

Disclaimer

The information contained in these pages and the route descriptions is provided in good faith, but no warranty is made for its accuracy. The contents are, at the time of writing and to the best of our knowledge, up-to-date and correct. However, the world is a changing environment and what is correct one day may not be so the next. Care should always be taken when following these route descriptions just as it should when following maps or waymarkers of any kind..

No guarantee whatsoever is provided by the author and/or Trailguides Limited and no liability is accepted for any loss, damage or injury of any kind resulting from the use of this book, nor as a result of any defect or inaccuracy in it.

As with all outdoor activities, you and you alone are responsible for your safety and well being.